Captain Wayne King

# From Cowboy to Game Warden

### Adventurous Short Stories From a Florida Game Warden's Career

**2**

**3**

**5**

## FOREWORD

In my 33 years as a judge working in the Fifth Circuit of Florida, I had the privilege of working with Captain Wayne King. His integrity was above reproach and his dedication, common sense, and reasoning were rarely equaled.

In the following pages are just a small number of the many fascinating experiences of Florida Wildlife Officer Wayne King. During his years working as a game warden, he engaged in many activities. From stakeouts on cold, dark nights to the recovery of lost loved ones who had fallen victim to drowning, these stories paint a picture of an exciting and harrowing career.

There is no typical day in the life of a game warden. He may be relocating an endangered animal, searching for a lost hiker by day, or chasing fire hunters at night. The next day may bring a boating accident investigation or the search for a child taken by an alligator. Next week, he may be assisting in hurricane recovery or restoring order to a city in times of unrest.

There is never a dull moment and each day requires a different set of skills and expertise to survive. He may be gone for 4 hours or 4 days. He spends most of his time alone in the vast Florida wilderness and backup may be hours away with no clue to his actual location. On land and on water, or in the woods miles from the closest road, he must rely on his experience and skills to safely return home.

If you want a taste of an exciting and fulfilling career, this book will provide one to you. If you want more than a taste, become a Florida Wildlife Officer.


Judge Hale R. Stancil, Senior Judge, 5<sup>th</sup> Circuit of Florida (Ret.)

Ocala, Florida

## INTRODUCTION

This book of short stories is part of the chronicle of my life as one of the last game wardens (by title) in the state of Florida. The true events described herein illustrate just a few of my many adventures enforcing the laws of the Florida wilderness. Through marshes and swamps, across rivers and lakes, and in the national parks and forests of our unique state, I attempt to bring you face to face with the realities of this exciting profession. I also discuss the thin thread that binds the survival of so many of our unique species.

From manatees to panthers, eagles to wild turkeys, these stories describe a 35-year career devoted to protecting and preserving the natural resources of Florida. My daily adventures were often humorous, occasionally disappointing, and sometimes dangerous but always brought a sense of fulfillment in knowing that I might have made a difference. This book is dedicated to those who lost their lives doing this same job (p.229), and to future generations who may enjoy the Florida outdoors as much as I have.

-Wayne King

## In the Beginning

In my life as an officer with the Florida Game and Freshwater Fish Commission (GFC), later known as the Florida Fish and Wildlife Conservation Commission (FWC), I lived through some very unique and interesting stories. On a daily basis, I encountered the humorous, the strange, the wild, and the dangerous. Throughout this book you can count on one thing: that the stories I tell you are of true events, whether funny, weird, stupid, or dangerous.

I think it might be interesting for you to hear some of the things that led up to my employment with the GFC.

As a child from a divorced home, I was raised by my grandmother. She instilled in me the value of hard work and effort. I spent most of my time growing up in the rural cow pastures of Florida, working cattle on horseback and learning to cowboy. By the time I was 15, I could break a horse and train him to do almost whatever I needed him to.

I started my career with the agency as sort of an afterthought. I married my high school sweetheart and entered the military when I was of age. I served four years in the United States Air Force, training as a jet engine mechanic. During that time, on deployment to Vietnam, I injured my spine in a hydraulic accident. My diagnosis was dismal. Doctors told me my injury would likely lead to paralysis and a life confined to a wheelchair within 10 years. With that perspective, I applied for a job at Embry Riddle University in Daytona Beach teaching jet propulsion. Then I got to thinking about how nice it would be to have some exciting memories and stories to tell while I was

**9**

sitting around in a wheelchair and couldn't get around.

I knew one of the lieutenants with the GFC in my home town of Bushnell. I had interacted with him several times while out hunting and fishing, and I always admired his job. I felt like it could be a pretty good gig. I enjoyed hunting and fishing and the thought of working outdoors seemed exciting to me.

I didn't really know exactly what all a game warden did, except for chasing people who didn't have permits for hunting deer, were illegally fishing, or occasionally killing a manatee. When I decided to put forth my application, a whole lot of people told me you needed to know somebody in the agency because it was very hard to get hired without a connection. Even though I did not have a contact in the agency, I was given an interview. I assumed the interview went well, as I was offered a job. They said, "Would you like to go to Dixie County?" I said, "Sure!", even though, at the time, I had no idea where Dixie County was, only fairly certain it was in the State of Florida. So, off I went, with my wife Marsha, to Cross City to begin my career. They gave me a badge and a gun and said, "Have at it." Actually, they gave me a badge. I had to buy my first gun. It was a .357 Colt. I also wasn't given a flashlight, a radio, or handcuffs. I had to buy all that later. We've come a long way to the body cameras of today. We also had no radio contact after 5 p.m. because the dispatchers went home for the evening, and no walkie talkie or hand-held radio issued to us. If we wanted to communicate with each other, we had to purchase and install our own CB radio.

Me, with my wife Marsha, shortly after
I entered the Air Force.

## "Learning the Hard Way"

I can remember the first day I reported for work in Lake City, where our main office was located, and got my first patrol car. It was a 1965 Ford. There was no cage for transporting prisoners to the jail. If I arrested someone, they rode up front with me. The car was nothing fancy and reminded me of something an old geezer fart would drive.

On my way from Lake City to Cross City, I encountered something I had never seen while driving on the road in Florida: my first red traffic light. By the time I realized what it was, I had to slam on the brakes and stop really quick. Unfortunately, the switch to operate the siren was located on the floor next to the clutch. When I attempted to stop by slamming on the brakes, I engaged the siren, making sure everyone around could see and hear my unfortunate mistake. Five minutes into my new job and I had almost been in my first traffic crash.

To make things more confusing, the blue light in my patrol car was not on top of the car like you see on today's patrol vehicles. It was a small tear drop light inside the car on the dashboard. It would frequently fall off the dashboard, especially during high speed chases. It would then lay flashing and spinning on the floorboard, making it difficult to see to drive the car for the blinding blue light flashing in your eyes.

My first assignment was in Cross City, which is about 6 miles north of the Suwanee River. I did some research on Dixie County before I moved there. Contrary to popular belief at the time, Dixie County wasn't just filled with ignorant rednecks who all hated game wardens. I was very blessed and fortunate to find the only person that would rent to me at the time, Marshall Clements. Marshall was a well-known person and well-liked as the Mayor of Horseshoe, a small fishing village on the coast of Dixie County. He rented me a lot next to his property, which enabled me to park my 10 x 47-foot trailer home.

Marshall maintained his own hog hunting claim, which led to him teaching me how to make country sausage. We kept a close friendship during my stay in Dixie County. Eventually, he was elected as a county judge and served as one of the last two judges in the state of Florida without a law degree. He developed a great reputation of fairness and impartiality, but dealt out justice in a way that changed Dixie County forever.

Years later, after I had been promoted and moved away, I would stop and have lunch with Marshall on my way to and from Tallahassee. I once asked him what made him decide to run for the judge's seat. He stated that his close relationship with me had opened his eyes to the injustice of game law violators in Dixie County and the importance and difficulties of the job we were doing. Judge Clements wanted to change the reputation of Dixie County and did so from the bench.

I hadn't been working long when they sent me a 12-foot aluminum boat with a 6-horsepower outboard motor. One of my primary duties would be checking boaters and safety equipment and looking for boating and fishing violations. This was very important since, at that time, one of the primary sources of income for the agency was the sale of fishing and

**13**

hunting licenses.

I'd never been on the Suwanee River before. I didn't know that it was as big as it was. The first boat I checked was about 45 to 50 feet long. It was considered a yacht. I didn't even know that yachts that big could get up from Florida's western coastline on the Gulf of Mexico all the way to where I was out on the Suwanee. It was over 30 miles up the winding river. It seemed sort of ridiculous to me as I pulled up to this ship, and from 10 feet below the top of the deck, hollered up to the captain.

"Can I check your life preservers, please?"

The guys up top laughed and stared.

"Are you serious", they mockingly replied.

"I think I can kinda see 'em. Just hold 'em all up."

They held them up and we laughed at the joke of a 12-foot jon boat checking a 50 yacht for life preservers.

I climbed up from my little boat to check his registration. At the time, I did not realize that vessels could be documented by the Coast Guard without being registered through the State of Florida. I wasn't trained or taught any of this. This was just the first in a never-ending line of learning experiences.

My first home was a small trailer that could be moved from place to place.

## *"Dixie County Lessons"*

Oddly enough, after six months in the field, I received my formal training. Training for the job was 2 weeks of school. It's humorous to look back on it, considering officers today receive 6 months of training in law enforcement certification, water and wilderness survival, and all possible aspects of the job, then receive 12 weeks of field training before being turned out on their own.

When I first started, game wardens only had the authority to arrest people on game and fish violations. Over time, that changed and evolved to include all aspects of law enforcement, leading to the modern state law enforcement officers we have today. They have the full authority of the State of Florida, and can investigate and arrest people for any violations of state or federal law they may encounter.

I learned many interesting things in training, but one lesson really stuck with me. At the time, we were told that we could only pull our weapon in self-defense. After the two-week training course, I asked David Swindell (the head of law enforcement training for the agency at the time) to clear up exactly when I could and couldn't, since I had already felt the need to pull it four times early in my career.

He explained it like this:

"If you walk up on a man skinning out an alligator, you know there's a violation and you know you're going to make an arrest. As you approach the man, he turns around and jams a frog gig into your stomach. What do you do?"

16

"Well, I know I can pull it then", I replied.

"No, you can't", he said.

"Only if the guy twists the gig. That way, you'll know he meant to stab you with it."

I always thought it was strange. I must wait for the guy who is stabbing me to twist the weapon, so I know he meant to stab me? It seems silly now, but that was the way of thinking at the time.

Cross City was a very unique place. When I arrived, a fresh new officer, most of the county was owned by the large timber companies. So, most of the rural landscape was planted pine trees. During this period, the state owned several wildlife management areas (or WMA's as they are known). These areas were set aside for hunting and recreation, much like they are today. These activities are allowed only during specified seasons throughout the year. However, in Dixie County, the rules were a bit different.

The people of Cross City and Dixie County were a very close-knit community. They all knew each other and were essentially one big family. I was the outsider. No one knew me, and they certainly had no use for a game warden trying to tell them what they could and couldn't do in their own backwoods. The way they saw it, the only things that were illegal were the things you got caught doing. To make things worse, there were around a dozen previous employees of the agency living in Dixie County. Most of them knew more about my job than I did at the time.

One afternoon, I was on patrol in a wildlife management area near Steinhatchee, a small fishing town near the Gulf of Mexico, just north of Cross City. I was driving down a graded dirt road in about 6 inches of water when I saw 3 dogs walk out in front of me. Shortly thereafter, I saw a horse's head emerge from the brush. On the back of the horse sat a man with a rifle in a scabbard. I knew immediately I had at least two violations of law taking place. Since it was not hunting season, the possession of a rifle and dogs in a WMA was against the law.

I was to his left and he was looking to his right as he entered the road. Oddly enough, he hadn't seen me and began to ride away from me following his dogs down the road. He was about 30 yards ahead of me, so I decided I would attempt to sneak up on him and grab the bridle of the horse to keep him from fleeing. Having worked with horses most of my life on the cattle ranches and farms where I grew up, I knew that if I could grab the horse's bridle, I could control the animal and prevent the rider from escaping.

I made it to within about 10 yards before he spotted me. He was startled and momentarily lost control of is horse. The horse began bucking and farting and just as I reached out to grab him, the man regained control of the horse and attempted to ride away.

I just managed to get a hand on the man's pants leg as he pulled away. I couldn't hold on and he quickly rode off as I foolishly chased him on foot. It turns out that even in relatively good physical shape, I couldn't outrun a horse. Given my injury, even though I worked very hard and long to manage and correct it, catching a fleeing horse was simply never an option for me.

I shouted, "Halt! Stop! Game warden! You're under arrest!" In hindsight, the only way I could have caught him would have been if he fell off the horse from laughing so hard at me.

Attempting to catch a horse-riding poacher while on foot is not the smartest thing I ever tried to do.

Dejected, I stood in the road for a moment and watched him ride away. Then I realized his dogs were still there! I took some crackers I had out of my car and I caught two of them. I placed them in the trunk of my car, determined to track down the owner. I drove back to an intersection about half a mile away, fairly confident that eventually the man on horseback would return. About 30 minutes later, two men in a pickup drove up. Neither was the man on the horse I had seen earlier.

"Hey, you seen our dogs around here? We lost 'em on our property while we was hog huntin'."

"Nope," I said, as the dogs in the trunk began to bark and howl.

"I thought you said you ain't seen no dogs", the man argued.

"No, I said I ain't seen **your** dogs. These aren't **your** dogs. You tell the owner he can come down here and meet me to get his dogs back!"

"You let our dogs outta that trunk or you'll get shot!"

In Dixie County, there were 3 things you didn't mess with: A man's guns, a man's dog, or a man's wife...pretty well in that order.

"You ain't shootin' nobody," I said, as the irritated men called on the CB radio for some friends to join them. I could see the confrontation escalating, so I figured it was probably time for some backup of my own. I called my partner in the area, Willard Bevel.

Willard was all of 120 pounds and very laid back. He became like an adopted uncle to me and I owe much of the success in my career to what he taught me in our time together.

After about 30 minutes, he showed up. He decided since these weren't the men I had been chasing and I couldn't prove the dogs were not theirs, it was in our best interests to give them their dogs back. I was disgusted and disappointed. I learned real soon that this is how things worked in Dixie County.

I also learned that most of the people in and around Cross City knew more about the laws than I did. Since they all knew each other, they also knew how to get around them.

A perfect example of this came about when I stopped a boat and issued a citation to the owner for having no registration. The boat wasn't documented or registered with the state, so this was as clear cut a violation as you would ever see. There was no question of his guilt. Instead of paying the fine, the man opted to take the case to court and have a jury trial. He was found not guilty. In Cross City, a jury of "your peers" meant a jury of your friends.

This was how all our cases went. The court would issue very small fines of $5 or $10, and the people of Dixie County knew that there was no real punishment for violating the boating, game, and fishing laws. This was very demoralizing to me. It didn't seem as though the courts were fairly upholding the laws. I felt like I wasn't making a difference.

I had several discussions with the local judge. We had developed a good working relationship. He was a big turkey hunter and I helped him find places to hunt and birds to harvest. I would take him to lunch and we would discuss the best ways to do our jobs. He told me that if he raised the fines, then people would simply go to trial and win. This would cost the court and the taxpayers more money than simply collecting the trivial fines the court had been issuing. Despite his advice, I lobbied for him to increase the fines, even if it were just to $15 or $20. He agreed to try it.

After a few months of cases, he turned out to be right. People began taking their cases to trial and being found "not guilty". After a while, the judge called me into his office and asked me what I thought was the best course of action. Again, feeling defeated, I agreed that the ridiculously small fines were better than losing every case. That was just how things worked in Cross City.

Many days and nights were spent walking in the vast Florida woodlands, searching for signs of activity.

### "Gun in the Gut"

I was still determined to do my job to the best of my ability. After a while, I began to learn how to deal with the people of Dixie County, and it often required some creativity on my part.

One day, while patrolling a timber area that was closed to hunting, I came across an elderly man in a car. I stopped him to see what he was doing in the area and immediately noticed a small .22 caliber rifle on the seat next to him. Again, possessing a rifle in a closed area is a clear violation. I asked him what he was doing with that rifle and he stated he was hog hunting. He ran a small hog trapping business and sold the hogs as meat. With the violation and his admission of guilt I decided to arrest him. As I reached in to take the rifle, he grabbed it, we struggled a bit and he jammed it into my stomach.

Normally, this situation would result in at least a fist fight, if not a shooting. In today's world, that man would likely be killed. I had to restrain myself from punching a 70-year-old man in face. I pushed the rifle to the side and said, "What are you doing? Gimme that gun!"

"No!", the man replied. "The last game warden that took my gun sold it to the pawn shop!"

"How do you know that?!", I asked.

"Because, I had to go down there and buy it back! Would you like to see the paperwork?"

Now, I figured that beating up or shooting an old man in Cross City probably wasn't the best way to befriend the community.

However, he was breaking the law and I had to take that rifle as evidence.

"You're under arrest and I have to have that rifle as evidence."

"Well, I ain't giving it to you! If you want, I'll take it to the Sheriff, but you ain't getting it!"

"Then you're taking it there right now!", I replied.

"Fair enough."

So, I followed the man to the jail and good to his word, he turned over the rifle into evidence. I issued him a notice to appear in court and we parted ways...and this is where the story gets interesting.

About a week later, I stopped the same old man in the same car, legally hog hunting. He had the same rifle! Considering that his trial for the first violation hadn't even begun yet, I was wondering how he got that rifle out of evidence.

"How did you get that rifle", I asked.

"I have a business trapping these hogs. I need the gun to work, so the Sheriff gave it back to me."

I went down to the Sheriff's Office and sure enough, the Sheriff had simply given the man his gun back. Once again, the rules didn't apply in Dixie County. However, shortly after that incident, I met both of the old man's sons. They were both well-known outlaws in the area. They introduced themselves, shook my hand, and thanked me for not hurting their father. In retrospect, I struggled with that decision. On the one hand, I could have easily been killed. On the other hand, I earned the respect of those men (and whoever they told the story to) by how I handled the situation. To this day, I don't know if I made the right decision, but it worked out nonetheless.

Officers working a typical
hunter checkpoint during a
busy hunting season

## "Off Probation"

After about a year of working, I was called to the regional office in Lake City to meet with my major. This was highly unusual as most things were filtered through the chain of command from the major down to the captains, the captains to the lieutenants, and the lieutenants to the sergeants and officers in the field. It was almost a 50-mile drive for me to visit the regional office and I rarely did so unless ordered to be there. Nervously, I made my way to the office.

When I arrived, the major took me into his office and asked me to have a seat. A little anxious, I asked what this was about. He told me he was trying to decide whether he could afford to keep me.

"What do you mean?", I asked.

"Well," he replied, "I get good reports on you but I just don't know if we can afford to let you keep working. You make good cases, but you recently broke your second patrol vehicle."

I had to tell him the story. I had recently been involved in a vehicle chase while attempting to catch some deer poachers late at night. When I attempted to drive across a small log bridge no wider than my car, I missed the bridge with the rear axle and broke the coil spring on my patrol vehicle. According to my major, no one had ever managed to break one of those springs before.

It turned out, he already knew the story. He was having a bit of fun at my expense and enjoying watching me squirm in my seat. He let me know he was happy with the hard work I was putting in, and he had simply called me in to congratulate me for completing my probationary employment period. So, with that little bit of humor, I was off probation and officially employed with the agency.

## "Snake Bite"

I was never fond of snakes. I know they serve a purpose in nature by keeping the number of pests under control, but growing up, a common saying in my neck of the woods was, "The only good snake, is a dead snake."

Obviously, working in the woods and on the waters of this state, it is a common occurrence to run into snakes, both venomous and non-venomous. Florida only has a handful of venomous snakes. The rest of them are harmless.

One of those dangerous snakes is the water moccasin, or "cottonmouth", so named because the inside of the snake's mouth is a bright white color. As its name implies, the water moccasin inhabits marshy areas around swamps, lakes, and rivers. They are well-known for their unfriendly disposition and a bite from even a small one is extremely painful and life threatening if left untreated over time. Native Americans who inhabited wilderness of this state knew that stepping on one was a good way to lose a foot, if not your life.

One day, during a long drought in North Florida, I was patrolling in the California Swamp area near Cross City. I had received some information that fishermen were taking hundreds of panfish from a large pond deep within the swamp. As the water levels dropped from the drought, the fish were concentrating in the pond, making catching them very easy. The limit at the time was 50 fish.

The only way to access the pond was on foot. It was over half a mile from the nearest road to the pond. I found a path with a couple sets of footprints heading towards the lake and it was clear they were dragging a small jon boat.

I set off towards the lake, hoping to get close enough to observe them without being spotted. As I waded out into the marsh around the edge of the lake, I caught a whiff of a very pungent odor. Immediately I recognized the smell.

Water moccasins, because of their diet, emit a very strong rotten smell, especially as they get bigger with age. I had walked right into nest of snakes. As I looked down around my legs, there were snakes everywhere. Several of the snakes were very large and irritated by me invasion into their home.

Standing in knee-deep water, I panicked. I drew my revolver and proceeded to fire all six shots into the mass of snakes. As I twirled and spun, I imagine I looked like a crazed gunman, blowing holes in the water at a frantic pace.

When the smoke cleared, I had hit precisely zero snakes. As they scattered, I took account of myself, making sure I hadn't been bitten in the ruckus. Thankfully, much like the snakes, I had no extra holes in me.

Then, I heard a voice not far off.

"Wayne? You aren't shooting at us, are you? We give up."

The fishermen I was stalking had witnessed the whole event, from the comfort of their boat. Thoroughly embarrassed, I responded in kind.

"No…no, just a couple snakes."

**31**

I couldn't hear them, but I'm sure they got quite a giggle out of it.

I didn't bother to wave them over so I could check them. I simply wished them luck and headed back to my car. After all, I was out of bullets.

## *"Hurricane Watch"*

One of the most important aspects of the job that most people don't usually consider is how we respond to natural disasters. Because of the specialized equipment we use, like airboats, ATV's, and four-wheel drive vehicles, we are usually the first agency on the scene in areas of destruction as the result of a hurricane.

I always found it hard to leave my family behind, while everyone else was fleeing from a storm, to head into the path of a hurricane. We leave our homes and our loved ones so that we can respond and help others.

I have known several officers over the years who lost homes and property during hurricanes, but still responded to disaster areas, putting their personal worries on hold, to help others.

As I am writing this book, there have been two major hurricanes make landfall in the U.S.

Hurricane Harvey has devastated parts of Texas with flooding, displacing thousands of people, and Hurricane Irma slammed into the Florida Peninsula, destroying thousands of homes and leaving millions without electricity and running water. A third hurricane, Maria, has taken aim at the Caribbean and Puerto Rico.

The agency has sent supplies and officers to Texas to aid in recovery, and our officers at home are working extra hours and days to help Floridians survive and recover.

In my career, I responded on scene to every hurricane to hit

Florida except for one. Our officers were vital in securing disaster areas and operating search and rescue missions for those stranded or lost in the storms.

Every year, hurricanes cause millions of dollars in damage and displace thousands of people.

## *"Booby Traps and Roofing Nails"*

Poachers have always been creative and clever people. They knew we were out there to stop them and we knew that they knew. So, we always had to be aware of our surroundings, especially in areas of high poaching activity.

One of the more insidious tricks they would employ was setting booby traps in spots that they knew we would be travelling. The traps weren't designed to hurt us, but rather our vehicles.

Several times, I found myself or other officers stranded in the middle of nowhere with four flat tires. You can plug one or two, but all four tires flat meant you were going nowhere fast.

The poachers would take a piece of lumber or conduit and drive nails through it. They would bend the nails over and hide the contraption in the grass or sand on trails and roads in hunting areas, knowing that when we drove over it, we'd be stuck.

I know this was meant to deter me, but it had the opposite effect. It just encouraged me even more. Not only were they breaking the law, but now they owed me a new set of tires. At times, I found myself taking it personally. I wonder if they ever considered this?

One of them took it a step further. There was a well-known poacher who I had had several run-ins with, and it was no secret that he hated my guts. I was always professional when dealing with him, but it just seemed like he always found himself on the wrong side of the law. It was also well known that he owned a local roofing company.

I guess he decided that he'd had enough. One night, I came home to find my wife upset, with four flat tires on her car, parked in our driveway. A quick inspection found all four tires riddled with roofing nails. I walked up the driveway to find dozens of them scattered around the entrance to our property.

I immediately knew who was responsible. Shortly thereafter, I arranged a meeting with the roofer. Much to his dismay, I made it very clear that if anything like that happened again, the resulting consequences would be unpleasant.

Thankfully, he became scarce after that, and we never had another problem. However, this was only one in a long list of issues my wife had to live through. It wasn't always easy being married to a stubborn game warden.

### *"Fighting Over a Deer Stand"*

One day I was patrolling the Citrus WMA during deer season, and was waved down by a hunter driving out. I pulled over and he wanted to share some information with me.

"There's two guys back there about to kill one another!"

"WHAT?!"

"Yeah," said the hunter, "They're arguing over something, making a ruckus about half a mile back. You can't miss it"

So, I hurried down the dirt road to the area the hunter directed me to. As I drove up, I could hear loud music blaring just through the blackjack oaks. Then, the music abruptly stopped. I heard some shouting and could see a vehicle through the trees, so I parked and walked to the men.

One man was sitting up in a tree stand, shouting and cursing at the man on the ground, who had driven his Jeep into the woods and was hooking a chain to the tree as I walked up. Apparently, he was going to pull the tree down, with the stand and the hunter in it.

I quickly separated the man's Jeep from the tree and tried to get to the bottom of what was happening.

The man in the tree stand had arrived to hunt. Unfortunately, he was sitting in the tree stand that belonged the man in the Jeep, and he refused to come down. In an attempt to dissuade the hunter, the man in the Jeep had set up a portable radio, and was cranking tunes in an attempt to ruin the hunt. I'm sure there was no need, as their arguing could be heard by every deer, turkey, and squirrel within a three-mile radius.

Undeterred, the bowhunter decided to silence the radio by putting one of his arrows through it. It wasn't a bad shot, hitting that small radio from 20 yards away.

Thankfully, after mediating the discussion for a few minutes and making sure neither man wanted to press charges, I was able to convince the hunters to move on and the two men parted ways.

It never ceased to amaze me the strange things you could run across in the woods doing this job.

Hunters usually place their stands near tree lines that form natural pathways used by game animals.

## "2 Car Chases, 1 Foot Chase, On the Way to Jail"

Back then, it was common for us to work fire hunting details using the agency plane. Fire hunting is when people in vehicles drive rural roads and shine a light to look for deer to shoot late at night. This practice is illegal, regardless of whether it's hunting season or not. As the hunters would shine their lights across fields and through cuts in the woods, the airplane pilot could see the lights from above and radio their position to us on the ground.

We would gather several teams of officers and spread them out over a large area. We worked in teams of 2 and would attempt to approach the fire hunters from behind with our headlights off to avoid detection. We would wait until the last possible second to turn on our lights and siren. Typically, once we were seen, one of the hunters would flee on foot with the gun or the light and the other would drive off in the vehicle. They did this to avoid a key component of the law which required that they be in possession of both the gun and the light for there to be a violation. Since it is damn near impossible to identify a fleeing individual running through the woods at 3 am, the hunters knew that if they split up they stood a better chance at winning in court.

I was partnered with Willard that night and the plane had spotted a light working a timber cut near our location. We quickly located the suspect vehicle and approached unseen. Willard was driving and as soon as we activated our lights and siren, the hunters held true to form.

The passenger jumped out of the moving vehicle and struck

out through the woods. He still had his light mounted on the top of his head and was carrying a rifle.

"Get after him, Wayne," Willard barked.

"Aren't you gonna stop the car first?"

"Hell no! Go on!"

So, out the passenger door I dove. As I bailed from the car, my foot slipped down into the rut in the sandy road and the car rolled over my boot. I jerked my foot out of the boot and took off after the fleeing hunter, who had nearly a 50-yard head start. I lost sight of him pretty quick since my flashlight kept switching on and off from the jarring and running through the brush. So, I stopped running and listened. I could hear him running through the woods like a deer, crashing and breaking branches along the way. I would chase him a bit, then stop and listen. Chase a bit, then stop. Eventually, he went to ground in some bushes and I caught up to him.

I called to the hiding poacher, "Come on outta there!"

"F--- you!", he returned.

Well, I was already out of breath, scratched up, and irritated...and I only had half as many boots as I started my night with. So, his response didn't help matters much. Into the bushes I went and grabbed the man by the light on his head. Unfortunately, in the struggle of pulling him out of the bushes, my knee smashed into his nose and broke it, completely by accident. At this point, he became compliant and we made our way back to the road.

As we sat there waiting for Willard to return, the man asked if he could have a smoke. I told him yes and asked him if I could have one as well. I didn't actually smoke, except for the rare cigar while I was in Vietnam. He gave me a cigarette and we waited.

Eventually Willard arrived, following the suspects' vehicle. It was a Volkswagen Beetle of all things, and they had broken off both mufflers and beat the car to hell trying to get away.

"Well, I got 'em.", Willard said.

In the old Volkswagen were two more fellas, the skinny driver and a heavy-set man in the back, who must have weighed about 350 pounds. Once all three were back together, they started to get mouthy and riled up. I walked over to calm down the guy I had chased through the woods earlier. No sooner than I turned my back, the other two had jumped back into their car and took off again.

We put my guy in the back of our car and took off after them.

Now, like I mentioned earlier in the book, it's important to remember that Willard was about 120 pounds and as laid back as anyone. We caught up to them after about a mile. Willard rammed the back of the Beetle and they stopped. Then, Willard hopped out before the car had barely stopped, went over to the Volkswagen (cursing and hollering the whole way) and snatched the fat guy (who was 3 times his size) right out of the passenger side door. Willard pulled him out to the ground and started kicking and stomping him for having the unmitigated gall to run, not once...but twice.

**41**

"You fat piece of sh--! I'll beat you're a--!"

I was a bit worried Willard might beat the guy to death, so I pulled out the driver, got the keys, and hurried over to pull Willard off poor tubby.

About that time, another officer arrived and we got things settled. We split the men up and transported them and their vehicle to the jail. I rode with the driver and fatso in the Beetle, and Willard and the runner went in our patrol vehicle. About halfway to the jail I hear the fat one talking to the driver from in the back seat. I didn't hear all the conversation, but I did pick up on a key part:

"...and when we get there, I'm going to cut off that asshole's head with this axe."

"What axe?!", I hollered back.

"This one here on the floor."

"Gimme that damn thing!" He held the axe up over the seat, right by the side of my neck. I took it and set it on the seat beside me. It wasn't me he was mad at. I wasn't the one who dragged him out of the car and beat him.

We impounded their now battered Volkswagen. It turns out, this was the first vehicle ever seized in Dixie County. Recently, the law had changed allowing us to pursue forfeiture of any vehicle or vessel used while fire hunting for deer or gators. Certainly, no one expected the first one to be a Volkswagen Beetle.

I found out during the trial that the man I chased through the woods had supposedly killed another boy when he was only 12 years old. He had slit the other boy's throat in a fight. He had also boasted to his friends that if a game warden ever tried to arrest him, he would "kill 'em"! Maybe my "accidental" knee to the nose made him rethink his decision.

### "My Life is Threatened...Again"

Towards the end of my time in Cross City, I received information from a man who had a falling out with his brother. I knew both of the men. They had previous run-ins with the law for beating some people up and one had even cut another person. They were both bad news.

He told me his brother was illegally trapping animals with steel traps. In North Florida, the weather gets cold enough that the animals put on enough fur to make the hides profitable. The problem was, the brother was setting his traps before the trapping season started, during the end of deer season. He did this to get a jump on the best spots.

This sort of information comes about more than you might think. Ex-girlfriends, wives who had caught their husbands cheating, relatives who couldn't get along...they all seemed to tell on each other when they were angry or upset at one another. So, if you were a hunter or fisherman who wasn't following the law at the time, it was in your best interests to keep your friends and family happy.

Anyhow, a day or two after receiving this information, the brother of the tattle tale showed up at my home. I was in my driveway washing my vehicle when he pulled up.

I walked over to the passenger side of his car and asked, "What can I do for you?"

"You got a minute?", he asked.

"Yeah."

It started to rain a bit so I had a seat inside his car. By this time, I was relatively well-known in the area and had developed a reputation as an approachable guy. I always found that it made my job easier if I was open to talking with people.

We were in my driveway no less than 20 feet from my front door. My wife was inside making lunch and probably overheard the louder parts of the conversation.

"I heard you have information about me steel trappin'."

"You did?", I replied. Of course, I would never tell him who gave me the information

"Well, I didn't come here to argue with you. I'm just lettin' you know that if you mess with me in the woods, I'll kill you."

It's a hell of a thing to hear someone tell you they'll kill you. It's another to have them come to your home and threaten you 20 feet from your wife and child. My initial thought was, "This must be the biggest idiot in Dixie County."

I got out of the car and walked around to the driver's door. I looked the man square in the face and said, "You get the hell out of my yard. If I see you again, in the woods or anywhere, I'll just assume you're there to kill me and I'm gonna kill you first. I'll just use a rifle and you'll never know what happened."

The man spun his tires and tore off down the road.

Later that day, I packed up a couple days' worth of sardines and a couple gallons of water and headed out to the woods, right where I knew his traps were. I sat on those traps for 3 days and nights. He never showed up. I fully intended to kill him if he did. I was in Dixie County another 12 months or so, and never saw him in the woods again. We were both probably fortunate that never happened.

I realize how crude and overly dramatic this sounds. In those days, working without a radio or backup, the job was extremely dangerous. When dealing with individuals like this man, it was important to understand how your words mattered. Any sign of weakness or hesitation could have meant the difference between life and death.

On page 229 of this book, there is a list of those who lost their lives in the line of duty. Their lives are a testament to the dangers associated with our chosen profession.

## "The People of Dixie County"

It was always my goal to treat everyone I encountered equally, whether they were well-known or not, whether they had money or were dirt poor. I think I developed a reputation of fairness in that community. While I was in Cross City, I not only arrested poor people just hunting and fishing for food and living off the land, but I also arrested some very influential people. I arrested a trial lawyer, a Methodist preacher, and even an astronaut.

My family and I had joined a church in Cross City. The people there were always friendly and except for a few people who I had arrested, they welcomed us into their church family. My wife even drove the church bus for a time, picking up the local children and bringing them to service.

When I decided to leave, the church threw me a "going away" party. The preacher, who also ran a timber company in the area, had two sons in their twenties. Both boys worked for the timber company and spent most of their time loading those logs by hand. I would imagine the two of them could have lifted a car.

At the party, he told me, "We are sad to see you go, but we're happy you're leaving."

"What do you mean", I laughed.

"Well, the boys and I have always loved fire hunting and when you joined the church I made them stop. We haven't been a single time since you joined. But now that you're leaving, we

**47**

just bought brand new lights and a box of shells. As soon as you cross over the Suwanee River and are out of Dixie County, we're going fire huntin' tonight!"

I was ordained as a Deacon in our small church in Citrus County.

## *"Leaving the Agency"*

I was raised by my grandmother. She was one-quarter Native American, so she was a tough lady. She had to be because I was an ornery kid, to put it kindly.

I'd been with the agency for a couple years when she became very ill and was hospitalized. I felt like I needed to be back at home with her, but I lived and worked over 2 hours away. I'd had always supported her since joining the military and the bills were piling up. At the time, I only made $360 a month working for the agency. I had been offered a job in Lake Panasoffkee as the co-owner and manager of a fish camp and lodge. My salary would increase to over $1,200 a month and it included a place to park our trailer home.

At the time, my wife and I had our first-born son, Dwayne. I thought at the time that this would be a good move for a short while, and my intention was always to return to the agency. I felt like this move would benefit my family, as my wife in particular had been through living hell in Dixie County.

I took a leave of absence for one year. I ran a Mercury outboard dealership while at the fish camp in Lake Panasoffkee. After about a year, I received a call from the Colonel. He had to put my leave of absence up for re-approval with the Commission and we knew it would not pass. At the time, they only granted them for educational purposes.

So, I went back to work for the agency. Since there were no openings, I did not return to Dixie County. I took a position in Citrus County, between Inverness and Lecanto. This area was much closer to home and it provided a whole new opportunity to explore different types of habitats and challenges. This created some exciting adventures and presented me with different types of outlaws than I had seen before.

## *"Citrus County"*

Citrus County was diverse and challenging place to work. It had a large variety of agency related activities and issues. Since it was bordered on the west by the Gulf of Mexico, it had both saltwater and freshwater commercial and recreational fishing. While the Marine Patrol handled most of the saltwater fishing and boating, we handled all the freshwater recreational and commercial activities. Citrus county has many freshwater bodies, including the Withlacoochee River, Crystal River, Homosassa Springs and Homosassa River, Chassahowitzka River and swamp, and Lake Tsala Apopka.

At one time, Lake Tsala Apopka, located on the eastern border of the county, was the second largest body of freshwater in the state behind Lake Okeechobee. This was prior to the lake being split into separate pools and marshes due to development and roadbuilding activities in the area. Most of these bodies of water were used for gator hunting, recreational fishing and boating, and commercial fishing. Although there were a number of small roads and trails separating the different parts of the lake, I could pretty well travel from place to place in my small aluminum boat, crossing the roads and trails when I needed to.

One of the more popular methods for fishing involved the use of trot lines. Trot lines were primarily used to catch catfish, but were occasionally used to illegally harvest game fish like bass, bream, and shell crackers. A trot line is a long main line tied to a stationary object such as a dock or a tree. The main line is run across a body of water with multiple smaller drop lines hanging baited hooks below it. The lines are set and left for several hours before the fisherman returns to harvest the catch. Trot lines aren't very sporting, but they are a very effective way to catch a large number of fish with minimal effort. This makes them popular with both commercial fisherman and those people who rely on the resources for food.

On the west side of the county, where all the rivers emptied into the Gulf, there were large communities of commercial saltwater fishermen. It was not uncommon at the time for them to travel upriver and set their gill nets to trap the fish in the confined space of the river. Even back then, this was illegal and I spent a great deal of time working these cases.

Citrus County also has a 30,000-acre WMA. This meant that along with the plethora of fishing and boating related challenges, I also had to deal with hunting and game poaching violations on a regular basis. Much like Dixie County, Citrus County had many dedicated hunters and well-known poachers.

All of these new challenges and experiences made for some very interesting and exciting stories from my time in Citrus County.

A long and lonely road to
the middle of nowhere

### "The Dog That Lived and The Gator That Didn't"

I hadn't been in Citrus County long when I received a call about a gator that had attacked someone's dog. This was a common occurrence in Citrus county due to the vast number of freshwater areas combined with the rapid development of homes and roads into and around those areas. As people encroached into the gators' environment, meetings between humans and gators became more and more frequent.

At the time, the agency did not employ "trappers", or people who were paid to respond to these calls and remove unwanted or dangerous gators. This meant that I would have to catch the gator myself. At the time, trapped gators weren't killed, they were relocated. Once I caught a nuisance gator, I would transport it to a wilderness area and release it.

On occasion, I would take an experienced person with me to lend a hand. So, this time I took one of my fellow officers by the name of Vernon Perryman. Officer Perryman had caught many gators and knew how to safely catch one.

We responded to the call and were surprised to learn that the dog, a large German shepherd, had survived the attack despite being cut up pretty bad. Most of the time, in that situation, the dog is never seen or heard of again.

Typically, to catch a large gator we would set out a baited hook attached to a gallon jug or a tree limb hanging over the water. We set the hook attached to a jug and retuned the next day. Sure enough, the gator had taken the bait and I could see the jug floating around out in the lake. So, Perryman and I climbed into my patrol boat and went out to grab the jug.

As we pulled this gator to the surface, it became apparent that the gator had tangled himself up in a trot line. As gators do, he had rolled himself attempting to escape only to wrap the lines and embed the hooks into his hide. I realized immediately that it was going to be a difficult and dangerous task to remove the hooks and lines from the now very angry gator. We got a rope around his neck and tied him to the boat, all 12 feet and 800 pounds of him.

As I was driving us back to shore, I told Officer Perryman,

"I have no idea how we are gonna get all these hooks outta this gator without him thrashing around and bitin' us."

Perryman frankly replied, "I know how!"

Right then I heard a loud "BANG"! I turned and saw that Perryman had shot the gator.

"Perryman," I exclaimed, "I didn't think we were supposed to do that!"

"Well," he said, "let the people who don't want us to kill them come out here and try and catch them!" As you can probably tell, Officer Perryman was a very colorful gentleman.

I figured this was probably the best solution at the time, seeing as how it was unlikely the gator would have survived the ordeal of being captured and having all those hooks stuck in him.

At least the dog survived. I think.

Alligators have been around since the dinosaurs and inhabit nearly all of Florida's natural bodies of water...as well as the occasional swimming pool.

## "Roadkill Deer"

Back in those days, we did not allow people to keep a deer they had hit with their vehicle. So, part of my job was to respond to those calls. When people called to report that a deer had been killed, an officer would respond, take the deer, skin it, and salvage as much of the meat as possible. The meat was typically taken to charitable organizations such as churches and old folks homes to help feed the poor and the homeless.

I was always opposed to this practice. It usually meant that an officer would end up ruining his uniform with blood and hair. On top of that, we were delivering uninspected meat to feed people, which didn't seem like the safest thing to be doing.

After nearly 2 years in Citrus County, I personally butchered and delivered over 40 deer as a result of road kills. Again, one can easily attribute the high number of meetings between cars and deer to the development of the area at the time. Although there are still plenty of deer in Citrus County, people have learned to be more alert and drive a little safer in those areas.

A typical roadkill deer, dressed and ready for donation to a local food bank or homeless shelter.

## "Smart Gator Hunter"

With all the freshwater lakes, rivers, and marshes in Citrus County, illegal gator hunting was a common practice. There were no such things as "alligator farms" back then, and in those days the population numbers were much lower than they are today. This meant that gator hides were more valuable, especially in places of high demand like Italy, where the hides were used to make high end purses and boots.

I had heard of a notorious gator hunter in those parts, and had run across him several times without finding any violations. As I understood it, he had been caught only one time, years prior, for gator hunting and had served a little time for it.

As with anything, the more you practice the better you get at it. Well, based on the reliable information I had, I knew this man was poaching gators on a regular basis. I just couldn't figure out how he was doing it without getting caught. Since he hadn't been caught in quite some time, one could safely assume he was pretty good at it. It turned out, he was exceptionally good at it.

There were several mysteries surrounding how he was able to do it. Every time we would stop and check his boat at the ramp, he was always clean. Where were all the gators he was taking? How was he getting them back to the hill (dry land)? How was he travelling between the marshes and dry islands and hammocks in the area?

Several times, I tried to follow him in my airboat from place to place, hoping to catch him red handed. I knew the area very well. Somehow, he continually eluded me. People like him were the most challenging to catch. They were also the most fun to pursue, so I dedicated a great deal of time to catching him.

One night, when I was certain he had been hunting I followed him, hoping to get close enough to catch him. Right before I was about to stop him, he ran his airboat up onto dry land into his back yard and right up to his porch. He hopped off the boat, carrying whatever cargo he had, and went right into his back door. I could not follow him into his home without a search warrant, so he got away again.

The man was incredibly shrewd and careful. He had taken large 50-gallon steel drums into the marsh and stashed them there. A steel drum with an airtight lid can be buried or submerged and would be impossible to find for anyone who didn't know its exact location. I only knew of one drum, but he almost certainly had several others.

He would then catch the gator, remove the hide, treat it with salt so that it wouldn't spoil, and then stash the hide in the barrels for what was sometimes weeks on end. He would then come back later, after scouting to make sure the coast was clear, to retrieve the hides. However, he wouldn't bring them back in his boat.

He placed the treated hides in large croaker sacks (brown burlap bags). He would then take his airboat to where the marsh was bordered by a roadway and toss the bags into the bushes along the road. He did this without stopping. He simply drove along the edge of the marsh and tossed them out, sometimes at 30 or 40 mph.

To keep us from catching him on the road in his car, he would drive to the area, stop, get out, slam his door – anything to draw attention and make sure no one was watching him. He would never go to the bags first, only to the general area. Once he was certain the coast was clear, he would retrieve the bags and off he would go.

Eventually, I decided that I needed to get a different view of the situation. So, I scheduled a flight in the agency's airplane, hoping to see something from the air that I hadn't seen from my boat. Airboat trails are easily spotted from above and I wanted to see exactly where he was going. I could see exactly where he had been. It turned out he was driving right through what I thought were heavily wooded hammocks. This puzzled me so I went back in my boat to get a closer look. I went to the hammock and got out of my boat to walk in, hoping to find some clues. I walked in about half a mile and what I found was surprising.

He had taken a chainsaw and an axe and cut a tunnel through the trees and brush underneath the tree canopy. The tunnel was just wide enough for him to pass his airboat through.

I knew that if I just sat there and waited on him, he wouldn't stop. He would either flee or worse yet, run me over. So, I decided that the best thing to do would be to put a large obstacle, like a log or brush pile, in his path and force him to stop so I could jump him.

I got it all set up, but about a month later I was promoted and moved. I never got the chance to go back and catch him. As far as I know, no one ever did. That's just the way it went sometimes.

My father in law, Bill Hutchinson, was an excellent gator hunter. I learned a great deal about how to trap and kill alligators from him. Here, he is taking a gator from its hole in a river bank.

I don't know that I have ever told this story before now. Mostly because people don't typically like telling stories about how they messed up. Thankfully, since I'm the only one with the agency who ever knew it happened, I'm the only one who can tell it.

One morning, I was sitting on the hood of my parked car in the middle of the Citrus WMA. I learned very early in my career that you could catch more people with your ears than your eyes. Instead of driving around and creating a presence, I would sometimes just park and sit...listening for a voice or a gunshot in the distance.

I hadn't been there too long before I heard a loud "POP, POP, POP". I knew immediately it was not a gunshot. It sounded more like someone banging on tree or a pole with a baseball bat. It continued... "POP, POP, POP".

On foot, I followed the sound about a half mile through the woods. I came upon two men. One man had a wooden axe handle and was beating the trunk of a tree with it. The other man, a little larger than the first, was dressed in overalls and wearing big leather gloves. He was standing about 10 to 15 feet from the tree. I watched them for a few minutes. "POP, POP, POP" The man would beat the tree while the other fellow just stood and watched.

"What in the hell...???", I wondered to myself.

Finally, I saw the man in the overalls grab at his chest and then

**63**

shove his hand into a bag. I couldn't stand it anymore. I had to know what they were doing. So, after I had snuck within about 10 yards of them, I said "Hey! What are ya'll doin'?"

Startled, they replied, "Catching flyin' squirrels."

"What?!"

"Catching flyin' squirrels. We take 'em and sell 'em down at the pet shop. We get like 2 or 3 dollars apiece for 'em."

"Are you serious?", I asked. I had never seen anything like that before. "How many you got?"

"Like 8 or 10.", they replied. Sure enough, the man in the overalls had a sack with about 10 flying squirrels in it.

Flying squirrels, contrary to their name, don't actually fly. They have extra folds of skin between their front and hind legs. When they jump from tree to tree, the flaps of skin spread out and they glide from one place to another, kinda like a parachute. They are also nocturnal and have huge eyes for such a small animal. And while they see well at night, they are almost blind in the daylight. They hide in hollow trees and nests during the day. They are very cute and docile. Another species similar to the flying squirrels native to Florida, known as "sugar gliders", are very popular as pets.

When the men found a hollow tree which they thought was likely to hold squirrels, the first fellow would beat on the tree to scare the squirrels out. When they attempted to flee, they would jump off the tree and glide to the nearest standing object. In this case, it was the man in overalls holding the sack of squirrels. Since they are almost blind in the daytime, they thought he was just another tree. When they landed on him, he grabbed them with his gloved hand and into the sack they went.

"You can't do that. It's illegal.", I told the men.

"Really? Well, we didn't know that!", they argued.

"Still, I'm gonna have to write you a ticket and take your squirrels."

So, I wrote the men their tickets and I took the squirrels. I opened the bag and out they all scrambled.

It wasn't until later that I realized I had screwed up. I was going through my codebook, looking for the exact law that covered flying squirrels. It turns out, flying squirrels, at the time this happened, were not protected. There are species of animals in Florida that aren't protected, like coyotes and wild hogs. Back then, one such animal was the flying squirrel. Once I realized that I had just arrested 2 men for a violation that didn't exist, I had the unpleasant task of calling them up and owning up to my mistake.

So, they agreed to meet me and I took back their tickets.

"What about our squirrels? What did you do with them?"

"I let them go."

"You let them loose!? What about our money!?"

I felt terrible, so the only thing I could do was give them some of the money they would have earned from selling the squirrels. I pulled ten dollars out of my wallet and handed it to them, hoping that they would never tell anyone this happened.

I learned that day to make sure that I read every law I was tasked to enforce. I had always read my codebook, but until that day, I had never run across flying squirrels before.

Flying squirrels are one of the most unique animals in the Florida wilderness.

## *"Gopher Tortoises"*

One of the more interesting and controversial animals we protect here in Florida is the gopher tortoise. A gopher tortoise is a land-dwelling reptile similar to a turtle, the main difference being that tortoises live entirely on dry land while turtles live mostly in and around water.

Gophers don't swim. They prefer high, dry, sandy areas. They like to dig their dens in the dry sandy soil. This means that north and central Florida are primary areas with large numbers of them. Citrus County was no exception. Citrus WMA was well known for its high density of gophers during my time there. Their dens also serve as shelter for a number of other species. One of those species is the diamond back rattlesnake. Many gopher tortoise poachers have found themselves face to face with an angry rattler when they poured small amounts of gasoline into a hose they ran down in a gopher den, hoping to gas out the unsuspecting tortoise.

Gopher are slow growing and have been known to live more than 80 years. Biologists suspect they could live to be 150 years old under the right conditions.

The gophers were also highly sought after as a delicacy by many people, especially the Menorcan people, whose ancestors were some of the first Spanish people to settle in colonial Florida near St. Augustine. Menorca is an island off the east coast of Spain. When they first arrived in Florida, the abundant tortoises were an easy source of meat.

One day while patrolling the WMA, I spotted a long-bed pickup truck driving down the roads that cut across the area. I watched two young boys hop out of the truck and run across a small cut in the trees. One of the boys was carrying a long pole with a heavy-duty wire on the end of it. The wire was bent into a "J-hook" shape. There was a woman driving the truck who turned out to be the boys' mother. I stopped the boys and asked what they were doing. They said that they were catching gophers. They were using the "J-hook" on the pole to pull the gophers out of their dens.

At the time, a full-size gopher would sell for between 3 and 5 dollars, which was pretty good money back then.

"How many ya'll got?"

"Oh, we got a quite a few," one of the boys responded proudly.

As I walked up to the bed of the truck, I was shocked to see more than "quite a few". The bed of the truck was completely filled with gophers. I estimated there were between 350 and 400 in the truck, all crawling and climbing over each other.

"Ya'll ain't supposed to be taking that many gophers outta here, even though they aren't protected. This is a wildlife management area."

"Well, nobody ever told us that!"

After learning my lesson from the great flying squirrel incident, I reluctantly sent them on their way. However, I was determined to put a stop to it.

A few weeks later, I was talking with the Chief of Wildlife in Tallahassee and asked him why the agency wasn't protecting gophers.

He told me, "Well, we are doing a study right now."

"Yeah, but they're taking hundreds of them," I protested.

Shortly thereafter, they were listed as protected. Originally, the limit was set to 5 gophers, then it was lowered to 1, and eventually they became completely restricted, making it illegal to take them.

I was glad to see the gopher tortoise protected. Between the loss of habitat from development and people filling truck beds with them, it's nice to know they still thrive in the Florida wilderness.

Thanks to the laws that protect them and their habitat, gopher tortoises thrive in Florida to this day.

## "Killing Bald Eagles"

I hadn't been in Citrus County long when I received a call from a biologist employee of the agency. They had found some eagles that had supposedly been shot by hunters. Given the protected status of the Bald Eagle and the reverence most people have for our national symbol, this came as quite a shock and was something I wanted to take care of immediately.

I went to the location where they said the eagles were and, sure enough, found 2 dead bald eagles. I immediately noticed 2 things: the eagles were intact and they had some slime coming from their mouths.

Since they were completely intact, it was easy to see they had not been shot. The slime from their mouths was typically a sign that they had been poisoned. Another clue was the location they were found. They were less than a half-mile from a large peach orchard.

I collected both eagles and sent them to a biologist to do a necropsy. This is like an autopsy in humans, but instead it's for dead animals. The necropsy showed that the eagles had in fact been poisoned by ingesting large amounts of DDT. At the time, DDT was a popular pesticide used by the commercial farming industry.

The eagles had been eating the rats, mice, squirrels, and snakes in peach orchard. As these smaller animals ingested the poison, it built up in their systems, and in turn, caused a buildup in the eagles' systems ultimately leading to their

**71**

deaths.

It wasn't long after that when the use of DDT was banned in the U.S.

Biologist were easily able to show the link between its use and the high death rate of many of the animals in the food chain, especially the top predators like Bald Eagles. This story just serves as another great example of the variety of issues I encountered while doing my job.

Florida's Bald Eagles are a great success story, showing how our agency and the public can work together.

Me holding a bird that
had been illegally taken.

*"Cuban War Games"*

Shortly after transferring to Citrus County, my wife and I found a quiet 5 acres that was less than half a mile from the Citrus WMA. This made it very easy for me to patrol the WMA on a regular basis. It was also centrally located to the main roads that ran throughout the county, making it easy for me to respond to calls efficiently, regardless of what part of the county they were in.

All this took place during the Cuban Crisis. Our government was in a political conflict with Castro's communist regime in Cuba. As a result, many Cubans had fled to South Florida. Many of these Cubans formed a militia in the hopes of returning to Cuba to remove Castro from power.

I was in the Citrus WMA when I came across three hunters. All three men were Hispanic, they all had rifles, and were dressed in full camouflage. However, when I started to question them, it became apparent that only one of them spoke any English. As I had them exit the woods, they placed their rifles on the hood of my car. I asked them for their hunting licenses, but they didn't have any. Using the one English-speaking man as an interpreter, I told all three men to follow me to their vehicle so that I could check it. Two of the men started to follow me to their car, but one of them quickly turned back and grabbed his rifle. I immediately drew my sidearm, fearing that I was about to be shot. The English-speaking gentleman, seeing what was happening, shouted to his friend in Spanish and asked me to stop. He told me his friend simply didn't understand and that he was merely being compliant. The man quickly set his rifle back down and the situation calmed.

I checked their car and found no further violations. I issued each man a notice to appear in court for hunting without a license. It wasn't until they appeared that I found out why they were in the WMA.

The men were not hunters. They were members of the Cuban militia who had come north from the Everglades to practice their war games for fear of being spotted or watched in South Florida. They were out in the woods that day practicing their war games.

There was never a shortage of strange and interesting things happening to me. You never know when world events might find their way to your back yard.

## *"Still No Eye Deer"*

Back in those days, it was a common occurrence for hunters, and just country folks in general, to find and collect baby deer, or fawns as they are called. When a fawn is first born, they have a hard time keeping up with the mother. So, typically the fawn will bed down and remain still while the mother wanders around to feed. Sometimes, a person would stumble upon the fawn and mistakenly believe that it had been abandoned. These people would often take the deer home in the hopes of raising it as a pet. However, this often resulted in the death of the deer from shock or malnutrition from being separated from its mother.

When this happened and we found out about it, we would take the deer and relocate it to a wildlife facility. The only such facility in Citrus County at the time was Homosassa Springs Park. The park was a privately-owned facility similar to a zoo. In addition to the springs, they had many different species of wild animal. The park was a very popular tourist attraction in Citrus County and remains open to this day. Part of my job was inspecting the facility on a regular basis to make sure that it was running within the laws and regulations set forth by the state. Today, the agency has inspectors whose sole purpose is to inspect the many zoos and attractions spread across Florida.

I was driving near the WMA one day when I spotted a small deer in the road. The deer did not run away. In fact, he stood motionless as a I approached. I got out of my car and slowly walked up to the deer. He still did not move. I waved my arms but he remained still. It became apparent as I reached him that he was blind.

I didn't want to leave him there to be roadkill, so I got the deer into my car and took him to Homosassa Park. Typically, they were happy to take in any displaced animals. This added to their display and would help provide more opportunity for tourists to view wildlife.

Upon my arrival, I was told that they would not accept the deer. When I asked why, they told me that tourists came to the park to see healthy animals and leave with a good feeling for the animals they had seen. They told me that a blind deer would cause the patrons of the park to be sad. They also said they couldn't afford to simply keep the deer in captivity and out of sight, feeding and housing it for the rest of its life.

Disappointed and without a second option, I returned home with the deer. I didn't want the deer to suffer any further, so I was forced to dispose of it. To this day, it still makes me sad. It was one of the more difficult moments of my early career and it demonstrates that not all of my adventures had a happy ending.

My oldest son, Dwayne, standing with the blind deer.

### "Homosassa Gill Netter"

As I stated earlier, Citrus County had quite a variety of fish and wildlife activities taking place on any given day. Typically, the saltwater fisheries and boating activities were overseen by the Department of Environmental Protection (DEP) or Florida's Marine Patrol, as they were more commonly known.

Occasionally, commercial saltwater fishermen would follow migrating fish species up into the freshwater rivers that flow into the gulf. Homosassa River is one such body of water. It flows from the head springs west into the Gulf of Mexico just south of Crystal River.

I had received a tip from one of the land owners who lived on the river that a well-known commercial fisherman (who was notoriously difficult to catch) was working a gill net under the cover of the late night and early morning darkness near the head of the Homosassa. The use of a gill net in freshwater is strictly prohibited. Back in those days, it was a misdemeanor. Today, it is a felony.

Mullet migrate up the river every year, and their large numbers combined with the small narrow confines of the river make them an easy target. A skilled poacher could net thousands of pounds of mullet in a matter of minutes.

I knew that approaching him in a boat would be nearly impossible, so I devised a plan to catch him from the shoreline. In order to avoid detection in the area, I used my personal vehicle. Commercial fishermen are a tight knit group, and I knew that if my presence in the area was known, I would have zero chance at catching the outlaw. I also needed to see him setting and working the net so that I could swear in a court of law that he had committed a crime. Once the fisherman had netted the fish, he would simply take the loaded net back to the fish house dock and, with the help of the dockworkers, pick the net clean. If this happened, I would have no case.

This all meant that I would have to get as close as possible without being seen or heard. I would approach the area in which I believed he would be working the net from land. I enlisted the help of a rookie officer, who would be hiding further down the river with a boat, ready to let me know when the outlaw was headed my way. When the poacher passed my lookout, I would be prepared to spring my trap. After the outlaw set his net, I would radio the rookie to cut off his escape and we could make the arrest. It was a flawless plan, or so I thought.

After several hours of waiting, and with no word from my lookout, I was just about to call it a night. It was around 4 a.m. when suddenly, through the darkness, I could see a shadow moving silently across the river directly in front of me. The silent specter was no more than 40 feet away. It was clearly a boat with one man inside, but there was no noise from a motor or even the splash of paddles dripping in the water. There was only dead silence, but the boat was moving up current at a steady pace.

Caught off-guard, I watched the man move across the river and begin to set a large net into the water. I was now certain that this was my poacher.

I waited and watched as the man set and retrieved the net and the fish trapped inside in complete silence. He then turned and silently head back downstream. I attempted several times to raise my partner over the radio, with no luck. I needed to warn him so that he could cut off the now escaping outlaw.

Worried that the radio was not working properly and knowing I had only a few minutes to spare, I quickly ran to a nearby payphone and called the landowner who had given me the tip. I asked him to run down to the river and alert my partner. He quickly made his way to where the rookie was hiding, and I made my way back to my vehicle and headed there myself.

When I arrived, I found the rookie and the poacher, who was now under arrest, waiting on the shore. Sure enough, the gill net and hundreds of pounds of mullet were in the boat.

"You didn't hear me calling you on the radio?"

"No," replied the rookie, "the radio must not be working."

More surprising though, was how the fisherman managed to move so silently through the water. He had wrapped the oars of his boat with burlap sacks. This meant that the water would quietly run back into the river as opposed to dripping noisily from the ends of the oars. It was an ingenious maneuver.

After securing the evidence, including over 400 pounds of mullet, and arresting the violator, I wanted to thank the land owner for helping us make the case. Without his help, our broken radios would have cost us that case. It turned out that my radios were working just fine.

"He was asleep, when I got down here," the landowner told me later, referring to my rookie partner.

"I woke him up just in time to catch the guy as he went by."

The rookie never would admit to it, but I had no doubt that the landowner was telling the truth. The officer had been dead asleep and of course never heard the boat as it silently cruised by undetected.

We seized the boat and the net, and after documenting all the evidence, donated the fish to a local charity.

The picture on the previous page shows a typical net being seized as evidence after the fish had been removed from it.

This picture shows the net with the boat, motor, and trailer. All were seized as evidence in the case.

## "The Great Bear Scare"

As previously mentioned, Vernon Perryman was another Officer who I worked closely with in Citrus County. He could always be counted on to lend a hand when I needed it. He had been with the agency for over 20 years and was a very hard working and honorable man. I learned a great deal from him.

One day, we were patrolling in the Chasowitzka swamp when we spotted a black bear high in the top of a palm tree. The bear was swaying in the tree back and forth.

I asked Vernon, "What's he doing?"

"He's getting something to eat."

The bear continued to rock the tree back and forth until eventually the entire top of the tree snapped off. The bear came tumbling to the ground with the top of the tree. I don't know how the bear managed to do this without getting hurt, but he seemed to manage just fine.

It turns out that one of a bear's favorite foods is heart of palm or, as it is commonly called, swamp cabbage. Swamp cabbage is found inside the tops palm trees and is the core of the growing tree. Many people (myself included) love to eat it. It is similar in taste and texture to chayote squash. It can be added to recipes, eaten raw, or used in deserts.

Seeing this reminded Vernon of another bear incident that had happened in the same area about 10 years earlier.

Vernon stopped his patrol car to get out and listen for shots or any activity. He hadn't been there long when he heard a high-pitched scream. He said it reminded him of a little girl and scared him terribly. So, he drew his revolver and set off in the direction of the noise. He hadn't walked very far into the bushes when a large black bear stood up on its hind legs. Vernon said the bear was at least 8 feet tall and had captured a squealing baby pig. The 15-pound piglet was in the bear's mouth as it stood no more than 10 feet from Vernon. Startled, the bear dropped the pig and ran. Equally startled and knowing his revolver wasn't much use against the bear, Perryman ran in the opposite direction.

Vernon was always full of stories and I always got a laugh out of this one.

It wasn't long after that when Vernon called me up and asked me to ride to our regional office in Ocala. His new patrol vehicle had arrived, and he wanted to know if I would ride up with him in his old car. He offered to get lunch on the way back. I couldn't say no. So, he picked me up at my house and we started the 40-mile trip to Ocala.

We got to the office, he signed all the paperwork, and transferred his gear into his new car. We were about to leave when he asked, "Hey, why don't you drive? I'm not used to driving in the city."

It wasn't uncommon for older officers to make the young kids drive and traffic was pretty bad in Ocala, even in those days, so I didn't think much of it. I hopped into the driver's seat and off we went. We had made it almost all the way back to my house when he said, "Turn down this road right here and stop."

Confused, I did as he said. We turned down an old dirt road that led into the management area. He got out and walked around to my side.

"Let me drive."

So, I moved over to the passenger seat wondering what he was doing. He got in, sat down, and then asked, "What do I do now?"

"Whatdya mean?", I replied.

"I've never driven one of these automatic transmissions before," he admitted, "so show me how."

There I was, a 25-year old officer showing a 60-year-old veteran how to drive his patrol car through the sugar sand in the middle of the woods.

### "Poaching Police"

One night, Perryman and I were on patrol together when we decided to park over a small rise in one of the many rural back roads in Citrus County. It was a week night and well after midnight. We took some small brush and branches and covered the chrome parts of the patrol car so they wouldn't shine if someone shined a light on the car. We hadn't been sitting long when we saw a car coming down the road, shining a spot light out the side. We knew this was a common area for fire hunting, so we weren't that surprised.

As the car got closer to us, we pulled out and blocked the road, turned on the blue light, and stopped the vehicle. Inside the vehicle were 3 men who, as it turned out, were police officers from a town a little bit south of us.

"We are just out looking at some deer." It wasn't illegal to shine the deer as long as you did not have a gun.

Perryman checked the car and got their I.D.'s.

"I didn't find a rifle," he said, "but you're welcome to take a look if you want."

So, I looked in the vehicle just to be sure. I spotted just the smallest part of something sticking out from in between the seat cushions. I reached in and pulled it out. It was a 12-inch .44 magnum revolver. I had never seen a handgun that big and didn't even know they made them.

We issued all three men citations for fire hunting and sent them on their way. It just shows you that you never know who you will find up to no good out in the woods.

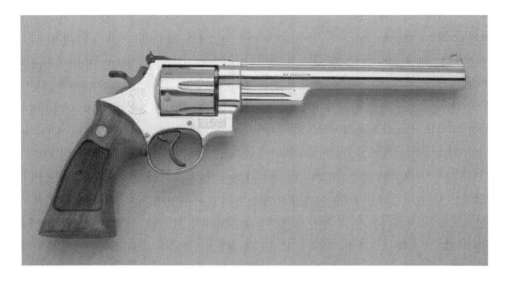

The .44 Magnum revolver
is a very powerful
handgun.

### "Spray Painting Mosquitos"

Sometimes the job was boring. It wasn't constant action and adventure. Most nights, the poachers just stayed home. But one of those boring nights turned into one of the funniest stories I had ever been a part of.

I worked with several unique characters over the years, and one officer in particular was always entertaining. He was a rather fastidious fellow. He had to have everything nice and neat, in its place, in order. He kept the inside of his patrol car in a constant state of cleanliness. He may have been the only officer I've ever seen with that specific habit. Heaven forbid you drop a cracker or a chip in his car. That was an act of war in his mind. We will call him Officer Tidy.

One night, myself, Officer Tidy and one other officer (who we will call Officer Prankster) decided we would get together to help break up the boredom of working fire hunters. The weather was drizzly and gloomy, and there weren't many, if any, cars out that night. We all loaded up into Officer Tidy's car and parked on a quiet secluded hill to wait for any shots or lights to pop up. Since it was raining, we could only crack the windows in order to make hearing a shot in the distance possible.

Cracking the windows meant that mosquitos could hunt us down. We were sitting ducks inside the car. Soon, all we could hear was the constant buzzing of the blood-thirsty swarm. In those days, mosquito spray was similar to cooking oil. Using it made you feel like a greased pig and it made you just as uncomfortable as simply letting the mosquitos bite you.

**89**

Eventually, it became too much for us, and we abandoned ship. Once outside the vehicle, Tidy decided he would fumigate the car with his can of mosquito spray.

Looking back, I wish Officer Prankster had clued me in on his plan. Sometimes, as with children, when officers encounter boredom it leads to mischief. What happened next was a disaster.

Officer Tidy proceeded to retrieve his can of spray from its designated storage location (which I'm sure was programmed into his brain) and unload it on the interior of his patrol vehicle.

Since it was dark and we didn't want to give away our position, Tidy had retrieved the can in the pitch-black darkness, assuming all along it was the mosquito spray he had so orderly placed in that very specific location.

About a minute into his extermination mission, Tidy began to cough and wheeze. As I walked back to the vehicle, the smell of paint was overwhelming. I realized that Prankster was laughing so hard that he couldn't breathe either. I had to know what was happening, so I turned on my flashlight.

Little did Tidy know, Officer Prankster had replaced his mosquito spray with a can of black spray paint equal in size to the can of mosquito spray. Officer Prankster just assumed that Tidy would spray himself, and at least 2 of us would get a good laugh out of it.

However, Officer Tidy had spray painted the entire inside of his car instead. The seats, the doors, the dash, the roof liner...even the windshield was covered. Officer Tidy had paint residue on his face, and his nostrils (now flaring with anger) were outlined in high gloss black.

For a moment, I thought there might be a shooting. Thankfully, between the paint fumes and the hysterical laughter, Officer Tidy decided against it. I assured him I was not in on the prank but, needless to say, we were never invited to ride with him again.

Early in my career, I learned a great deal from the officers who came before me.

I am seated in the middle of the back row.

## "Another New Beginning"

After several years in Citrus County, I had become very comfortable as part of the community. Most of the people in Citrus County were very welcoming, and I had developed a reputation as a fair and honest game warden. It got to the point where, if I wanted to, I could just sit at my home and wait for the phone to ring, then go out and make an arrest. I didn't do this, of course, but you get the point.

People in the community knew me and would often give me information about violations they observed or knew were taking place. I had to take this information very seriously because if the people I was arresting knew how I had found out, they could have potentially sought revenge on the informants. There were examples in the past of houses being burned down and in some cases, lives being threatened or taken. I even had a father turn in his own son for a poaching violation. At the time, I struggled to understand why the father did it. Later in life, it became clearer to me. I once wrote my oldest son a warning for taking too many ducks on a hunting trip. It seemed like the right thing to do and would have been how I treated any member of the public. To this day he is still upset with me over that.

Around this time, I received the opportunity to promote within the agency. So, I took the test and passed. I was promoted to sergeant. My new area would consist of Polk, Hardee, and north Highlands Counties, the Kissimmee River and Lake Kissimmee.

I knew when I promoted that my job would change from

making my way on my own to supervising a group of officers. At the time, the vast majority of officers with the agency were highly motivated and good people. This wasn't always the case and it would now be my job to manage some of these people and help point them in the right direction. Everybody did things a little different.

As we move forward, I will not always be the arresting officer in the story. However, I was directly involved in each and every case as part of the investigating team or as the supervisor (sergeant, lieutenant, and eventually captain), making sure that we were doing the right thing. I wasn't always on the scene when things happened, but I was directly responsible for these cases and the people involved.

In deciding which stories to tell and which ones to leave out, I also considered the status of this profession in the public's eye in present day terms. As a supervisor, I wanted all of my officers to give "100%". For the most part, they did. But like any profession, law enforcement has its bad apples. Occasionally, an overzealous or thoughtless act resulted in a situation that cost someone their job, or worse, the loss of a life. One needs only to turn on the news on any given day to see the mistakes made by law enforcement officers across the nation. These mistakes are often magnified and publicized in the media, for better or for worse. Every American carries a cell phone with a high definition camera and the ability to shoot their own live action film at a moment's notice. The reality of this job means that our mistakes are what define us in the eyes of the public.

It is for this reason that I left out most of the stories involving the more serious mistakes made by my officers. I've included many of my own mistakes simply to illustrate a lesson learned or to add humor to serious situations. While I don't mind illustrating my own failings, I don't want to bring publicity to the failings of others, especially those still working and living in this state, or their family members.

My first wife, Marsha, and our two sons, Dwayne and Levi.

## "Houseboat Outlaw"

Early on, in the area of Lake Kissimmee, I received a tip that there was somebody on a houseboat illegally trapping fish. Houseboats are exactly what they sound like: a small house or apartment built on top of a boat hull, usually a deck boat or pontoon boat. They are complete with a roof, doors, and windows. Some of them even have air conditioning these days. The structure on the boat makes it impossible to see what is happening inside the vessel.

There were several houseboats on the lake and I wasn't sure which boat it was. After several days of surveillance on the lake, I noticed one boat acting strangely. It would travel to and from different spots on the lake repeatedly, stay there a short time, and then move on. The boat did this over multiple days. I didn't see anyone on the boat fishing so I couldn't understand why it was constantly visiting the same spots over and over again. I decided to stop the boat and investigate further.

At the time, we could search boats, cars, or property if we saw, heard, or smelled anything that was reasonably suspicious. When I stopped this boat, he had a lot of bluegill bream on board, more than could be caught by one person with a fishing pole in a short time, but there was no sign of any traps. As I inspected the boat further I noticed something interesting. There was one spot inside on the floor of the boat that was very wet. The boat was completely enclosed, so there was no reason for it to be that wet.

Upon further inspection, it turned out to be a trap door in the bottom of the boat. The man was driving the boat to his traps,

**95**

opening the trap door, and emptying the traps inside the enclosure. He would then reset the traps and move on, completely concealed and unseen from the outside. It was quite literally a "trap door".

After watching him for all that time, it was easy to locate all his fish traps on the lake. I just had to revisit the spots he frequented while I had been observing him. I have always been amazed at the ingenuity and the lengths people will go to break the law. Although his methods were relatively simple, they were incredibly effective.

Wire fish traps, typically used by commercial fishermen and poachers alike.

## "Fishing Licenses"

One of the most routine things wildlife officers do is check fishing licenses. At the time, I thought I was pretty good at picking out which people were most likely to not have a license. So, as a new supervisor, I took it upon myself to help those officers who had a harder time catching people who were fishing without a license. Confident in my skills, I partnered up with one of my officers and we went out on his patrol boat. As we usually did, we would stop boats and check fishermen and their catches, or pull up to shore and check people fishing from the bank.

We spotted a father and son fishing along the shore and pulled up to them. As I got closer I realized the boy had his rod and reel propped up with a stick on the shore. No sooner than I saw it, it bent over and shot out into the river. Initially I thought that a large fish was on the other end. Then, his father shouted at me.

"You've got his rod!"

What had happened was, as we pulled up in the boat, his line had become tangled in the prop and then broke off. The boy was understandably distraught and his father wasn't all that happy with me either. Embarrassed, I unsuccessfully looked for the boy's fishing pole for a good 30 minutes before I realized what needed to be done.

I asked the father if they would be there for a while longer. He said that he would. We loaded up the patrol boat and in to town I went. I stopped at the local K-Mart and bought the boy a new rod and reel, making sure it was nicer than the one I had lost him. I also bought him some fresh bait. I returned to the spot where they were fishing and the boy was as happy as he could be to get a brand-new rod and reel.

It turns out I wasn't as good at checking fisherman as I thought I was. I learned a good lesson that day and a little humility in the process.

In good weather or bad, the waterways still needed patrolling. If it was cold and windy, you wore a jacket, but you went anyway.

**"Dodging Catfish"**

Known for its role in Florida's cattle industry since the Civil War, Lake Kissimmee in Osceola County is a popular recreational and commercial fishing area. It is also a popular place for poachers and outlaws to work under the cover of the remote Florida darkness.

I spent many nights on foot, in my patrol car, and mostly, in a boat, quietly making my way around Lake Kissimmee and its surrounding wilderness. Over the years, I chased and caught numerous outlaws killing gators, taking too many fish, and fire hunting deer. However, one case in particular sticks out in my mind, not because of what the man was doing, but more so because of his attempt to escape and the lesson I learned afterwards.

After a long and uneventful evening floating slowly around the lake in my patrol boat, I was almost ready to call it a night when I spotted a boat with no lights, silently idling across the lake a few hundred yards away. Even though there was only a sliver of moon that night, I could see the wake of the boat reflecting the starlit clear sky. There was no wind and the surface of the lake was as smooth and reflective as a polished mirror.

I had received several complaints of illegal fish trapping on the lake, and I was certain I had just run across my first case. I slowly followed the boat at a distance and could clearly hear the man inside rattling the fish traps as he pulled them from the water and emptied the contents into the bottom of his boat. After I listened to him pull and empty four or five traps, I decided it was time to take him down. I got as close as I thought I could without being spotted and lit him up. Immediately, he dropped a trap back into the water and the chase was on.

As I got closer to his fleeing boat, it became apparent that there was nowhere for him to go and no way he was going to outrun me. What he did next was slightly dangerous and incredibly entertaining.

I watched the panicked man reach down into his boat with one hand while holding onto the controls of his boat with the other. Fearing he may have been reaching for a weapon, I readied myself and reached for my sidearm. Then, the man made a short throwing motion, reached down again, and repeated the same motion. At first, I could not figure out what he was doing.

Then, a loud "SMACK" sounded from the front of my center console. Then another...and another. Then, as it barely missed my head, I caught a glimpse of what the man was throwing at me: his catch.

The man continued to hurl catfish, one after another, at me as I approached his vessel from the rear. A catfish to the face would be an incredibly unpleasant event. Realizing that not only were the barbed slimy fish a danger to me, but that he was also dumping my evidence, I quickly brought my boat alongside his. My first thought was to shoot his engine and bring his boat to a stop, but then I worried I might accidentally hit the man. So, I yelled to him in the harshest voice I could manage:

"You better stop or you're going to get shot!"

My bluff worked. The man relented and pulled back his throttle, settling the boat idly alongside my own.

The case was simple. I had observed the man with trap in hand, and his boat still contained about a hundred pounds of live catfish...minus what he had thrown my way. It seemed like an open and shut case, or so I thought.

Because of the pitch-black darkness that night, I had never actually seen the man empty the fish from the traps and there was no way I could swear under oath that the catfish in his boat came from the traps. Just like that, "case dismissed".

However, I did learn a very valuable lesson, which led to a foolproof strategy for working such cases in the future. From then on, whenever we worked fish trapping cases, we would first find the traps. Then, we took sewing pins and placed them under the skin on top of the catfish's head, and placed him back in the trap. Once we caught the trapper in the act, it was a simple matter of running a metal detector over the pile of fish in the boat. Once we found and documented the pins we had placed in the trapped catfish, it was game over for the trapping outlaw.

Dodging catfish in the dark while trying to chase an illegal fisherman was a memorable experience.

### "More Alligator Trouble"

At the time, alligators were still protected and hunting or possessing them was illegal. I was walking through a market one day, when I noticed several pairs of very expensive boots that were made of alligator skin. Knowing that this had to be illegal, I seized the products and issued a notice to appear in court to the store manager.

At the time, we only had one biologist who was an expert on differentiating between gator skin and the skin of a caiman or a crocodile. When I contacted him, that biologist was sure he could tell the difference. Upon looking at the boots, he was certain they were gator skin.

Right before the trial, the biologist changed his mind and said he couldn't swear under oath that the boots were alligator skin. So much for my case. It was dead in the water.

Embarrassed, I returned to the store to let the owner know what had happened. I let him know they couldn't sell the boots anymore and they agreed not to. I tried to return the boots but the store owner did not want them back.

"If they're illegal and I can't sell them, I don't need them in my store!"

I couldn't keep them or dispose of them without a court order. Since I had a good working relationship with the judge, I asked him what he wanted to do with them. He said that he knew exactly what to do with them. He would donate them to the Rodehever Boy's Ranch, a charity home for troubled young

**103**

men.

It was really entertaining to see these young boys, many of whom lived most of their lives in poverty, walking around proudly in their new $500 alligator skin boots.

Another incident, that again proves you never know what you'll encounter doing this job on a day to day basis, involved a prison guard in a county to the south of my supervisory area. Apparently, in his off-duty time, this guard was selling alligator hide products, such as belts and wallets. It became obvious that he was poaching the gators, but after weeks of following and observing him, we found no evidence of him hunting the gators. We simply could not figure out when and where he was hunting the gators and taking the hides.

After what seemed like a year's worth of frustration, we finally had an epiphany. The reason we could not catch him in the act was because he was hunting the gators in the one place we could not observe him: the prison. There were several retention ponds and marshy areas on and around the grounds of the prison. He was hunting the gators while on the night shift, while he was on duty. What eventually led to his downfall was the fact that he was using one of the inmates to tan the hides and prepare them for sale. He was hunting, preparing, and storing the hides all within the prison itself. We were never able to observe any of this happening but did receive testimony from witnesses inside. Due to this, we could never bring a strong case against him, but we were able to put an end to it and the department of corrections handled the matter internally, ultimately removing the guard from his position of employment. We all know prisons are filled with criminals, but you typically don't find many gator poachers actively working within the prison.

## *"Alligator Ride"*

Another story about a nuisance gator I had to catch ended with me getting knocked unconscious. I responded to the call of a nuisance gator and as usual, put out a line and caught him. The gator was about 7 feet long and pretty heavy for that length. I had to wrestle with him for a few minutes before I was able to subdue him. I took my handcuffs and cuffed his front legs behind his back. I taped his mouth shut and put him into the trunk of my car.

I intended to transport him to a rural area of the Kissimmee River and release him. I was filthy and the gator had peed all over me while we were wrestling, so I decided to stop at the house to wash off and grab a bite to eat. I got to the house and thought it best to open the trunk so that the gator wouldn't get too hot. I didn't think he could climb out of the trunk with his hands cuffed. I was mistaken.

I had just hopped out of the shower when I heard my wife holler, "Your gator's loose!"

At the time, we lived on a piece of property right next to a phosphate pit. If he had made it over the edge of the pit, I would have lost my handcuffs and he would have eventually drowned.

I ran out the door and hopped on the back of the gator. Gators are well known for their death roll. They grab ahold of their prey and roll, breaking and tearing whatever leg, head, or arm they chomped down on. The only way to prevent this is to jump on their back and pull their head back. His mouth was taped so I wasn't worried about getting bit. The other thing gators are known for is using their enormously strong tails as weapons. They will bend their head and body while simultaneously whipping their tail, causing whatever unfortunate animal is in the way to be knocked into their jaws. I wasn't prepared for this maneuver and the gator's head snapped back and hit me directly in the top of my head, knocking me out. I came to only to find I was being pummeled by the fat gator. Still dazed and barely conscious, I wrestled the gator as best I could, but the gator was more up to the task than I was.

Thankfully, my wife saw the whole thing. Watching the gator beat me to a pulp with its tail, she ran out and pulled me out of harm's way.

I learned a good lesson that day: Don't use your handcuffs on a gator.

After I recovered, I delivered the gator safely to the Kissimmee River. I assume he lived a happy life, telling all his friends about how he beat up a game warden making his daring escape.

One of the gator's natural instincts is to throw its head and tail together to force its prey into its mouth. Unfortunately, my face took the full force of this maneuver.

## *"Dragline Destruction"*

In the latter half of the 20th century, development in Florida was at a fever pitch. The coastline and surrounding wetland areas were being decimated by dredge and fill operations. Developers used draglines to dig canals, drain marshes, fill in areas for development. This also had a drastic and destructive effect on inland waterways, lakes, and springs.

During this period, there was no Department of Environmental Protection. So, there really was nobody enforcing the regulations that these dredge and fill operations were supposed to follow. There was nobody protecting the state lands and waters.

One day in Highlands county, I happened upon a dragline working, digging a canal. He was digging right in the waterway, which was a clear violation. So, I gathered all the information, took some photographs, and issued the citation. At the time, it was only the second dredge and fill violation case in the history of the state of Florida.

If you look at the east coast of Florida especially, you can see how this type of development shaped the state and caused land values to skyrocket. There were a lot of people in positions of power involved in development and a lot of money to be made.

As I moved forward, the assistant state's attorney, who was a private lawyer under contract with the state, took the case. After about a week he called me back and told me that he was recusing himself from the case. It turned out, he was a stakeholder with the company that owned the dragline. The case ended up being dropped because of this.

I was disappointed but not deterred. Those types of operations were destroying the waters of the state and I was determined to do what needed to be done to protect those resources. I felt like most people at the time weren't looking at the big picture. If this type of development continued, there would be no places to fish, no places for wildlife to live and drink. I became very dedicated to this task throughout the rest of my career. It was my hope to protect the woods and waters of this state which the fish and wildlife needed to survive and thrive.

Draglines are used to create drainage canals and retention areas, clearing large areas of wetland for developers.

Florida's rivers, lakes, and
marshes are vital to the
survival of all the flora and
fauna of the state.

## "Tammy Wynette and George Jones"

As a law enforcement officer in Florida, you interact with all sorts of people from every part of society. Obviously, you spend time dealing with criminals and law breakers, but a big part of our job is public service, outreach, and education. This means that you never know who you are going to meet. I met a great number of famous and influential people over the years.

While I worked as a sergeant in Polk County, I had the opportunity to meet Tammy Wynette and George Jones. For anyone reading this who may not know, George and Tammy were very famous and well-known country music artists, both of whom are in the Country Music Hall of Fame. They owned a home and amphitheater in the area, and though they have since passed away, they remain icons of their industry to this day.

I received a call one day about some shots being fired on their property and possibly some illegal hunting going on. I responded and found it was just some people target shooting. There were no hunting or game violations taking place. It was just some fellas having a little fun.

Of course, George and Tammy were curious about my arrival and the situation, and after I assured them there was no problem, we had a pleasant and lengthy conversation. They invited me to stop in and visit any time I was in the area. I was more than happy to do so. Tammy was an excellent cook and her chicken and dumplings were one of my favorites. So, every chance I got, I would drop by to visit my new friends.

I was excited to be socializing with two popular celebrities and they were interested in my job and any information I could give them on fishing in the area. In turn, I was curious about their travels and stories from their decades in the country music business.

It turned out that they loved to go catfishing, and pressed me to clue them in on the local hotspots.

One day, George asked me, "I really would like to go catfishing. Do you know a good spot where Tammy and I could go?"

"Of course!" I knew the perfect place.

Being so close to the Kissimmee River, I knew of a private ranch that would be an excellent place for them to go. It would offer them a quiet view of the river and ensure they wouldn't be disturbed by anyone who might recognize the two famous singers.

So, I got permission from the land owner and we made the plans to go. Oddly enough, they packed up their things in a tour bus and I followed in my own personal truck. We pulled into the ranch around dark, and it was raining just a bit. The spot was a beautiful oak hammock that sat on the bank where the river bordered the ranch.

We decided to set a trot line, so we got all the gear set up just in time to see it start raining buckets. It must have rained 2 inches in just a couple hours. We decided it would be best to wait inside the bus.

Now, in my defense, I had only considered the privacy of the ranch as a benefit to George and Tammy. I wanted to make sure they enjoyed the fishing and that they knew they could count on me to help them out. What I had not considered was that the ranch was filled with hundreds of cattle (obviously, since it was a cattle ranch). Apparently, this particular oak hammock was one of their favorites, as evidenced by the never-ending amount of cow poop on the ground.

So, there we were in the dark and pouring down rain, in a cow pasture which was quickly becoming a soupy mixture of dirt and cow manure. To make matters worse, we were tracking in and out of a $200,000 tour bus every time we went to check the trot line.

"I'm so sorry about this," I humbly explained.

"Don't be," said George, "we're having a great time."

If I remember correctly, I think we caught 2 fish the whole night. It wasn't exactly how I had envisioned the trip would go.

George and Tammy were two of the most down to Earth and humble people I ever met. It was a privilege just to sit and visit with them that night, even if it was in the middle of a flooded cow pasture, during a typical summer downpour.

### "Airboat Chase Number 1"

Airboats are a great way to get around the wetlands of Florida. The boats are run by a large car or aircraft engine mounted on a steel cage above the hull. The engine drives a large-blade propeller, much like the one found on an airplane. Airboats can run in the shallowest marshes and swamps and, given the correct setup, an airboat can even run on dry land.

One of my favorite things to do was work late at night on a Friday in my airboat. I would take my boat to a private ranch on Lake Kissimmee well after dark so I could launch undetected. Friday nights were popular with gator and deer poachers who had worked all week and just got paid. They would have a couple beers with their buddies after work and head out to run their airboats to see what they could find. I had recently found some remnants of gator carcasses in the area and I knew there was some illegal activity taking place.

Usually, I would take one of my officers with me. However, this night the partner I was supposed to have got sick at the last minute, leaving me to fend for myself.

It was early in the morning around 3 a.m. and I was sitting on the boat in the pitch-black darkness waiting for some action. Eventually, I heard an airboat headed in my direction from across the lake. As he came into view about a half mile away, I could see he was working a spotlight from side to side, shining it on the water as opposed to out in front of the boat, towards his direction of travel. This told me that he was fire hunting for gators. At night, an alligator's eyes will reflect a spotlight, producing a very bright signal that gives away their location.

**115**

They might as well wear neon signs on top of their heads.

Abruptly, the boat slowed and the driver killed the engine. Seconds later,

**"POP"**, one shot.

They had shot the gator! In the light they were working, I could see two men moving around and pulling the gator into the boat.

I decided to wait until they had loaded the gator and started back up before I cranked my boat and went after them. I also wanted to make sure that airboats are loud and any signal that would have given away my presence would have alerted the men, who already had a significant head start. Once they knew I was there, they would immediately dump the gator, the gun, and other evidence of their crimes. So, I would wait until I was sure they were headed away from me.

Eventually, they started back up and I did the same. It was important for me to maintain a constant speed in pursuit. Any variation in the throttle of my engine would change the volume and pitch of the noise my engine and propeller produced.

As I slowly closed the distance between us, I was careful to follow and observe as they continued to hunt. I knew that once I made my move, they would likely dump the gun first. A popular tactic to counter this move is to use a marker buoy. I white gallon jug attached to a line with a weight at the end works perfectly. When in a boat chase, if the offender decided to throw anything into the water, I would have the buoy ready to deploy, allowing me to come back to that exact location later with a drag hook and line to retrieve what they had thrown out.

Just as I had gotten close enough behind them to see them relatively well, the driver working the light spun his head around and spotted me.

The chase was on!

We immediately reached speeds of 50 to 55 miles per hour. In an airboat at night, this is extremely dangerous. The chase went on for 20 minutes or so before the situation got worse.

I hadn't done my homework. I was familiar with the lake but hadn't paid attention to where the cattle ranchers had placed their fences. When water levels in the lake drop, the ranchers build barbed wire fences out into the lake to prevent the cows from going around them and escaping. Typically, when the water levels came back up, the ranchers would just leave the posts, essentially creating an artificial stump-lined mine field for any unfortunate boater unaware of the obstacles.

At the speeds we were traveling, hitting one of those posts would almost certainly cause the boat to roll completely over and crash, resulting in the likely death of anyone onboard.

Just as I approached the fence, I saw the barbed wire in my light. It was high enough out of the water that it cleared the deck of my boat and struck the framework just below my driver's seat. If I had been carrying my then sick officer as

**117**

planned, it would have at least cut his legs off, if not much worse. Thankfully, the wire snapped I was able to continue the chase.

Eventually, I managed to get the poachers stopped. As predicted, they had dumped the gator and the gun. The only evidence on the boat was the blood of the gator. And even though I managed to get one of the men to fess up, I lost the case in court due to a lack of evidence.

Even though it was an exciting chase, and no one was hurt, it demonstrated how easily things can go wrong and how dangerous working on the wetlands can be.

An airboat is an essential tool for traversing the marshes and waterways of Florida. It allows us to get to places no other vehicle or boat can go.

## *"Officer Tree Monkey"*

Early in my career as a supervisor, I made a habit of getting to know my officers as well as I could, just to get a feel for how they worked and to make sure they knew if they needed anything, I was always available to them.

I had a young officer in Hardee County who I had never worked with before and I decided that I would go with him on a fire hunting detail to see how he was doing. We met for dinner one evening and shortly after dark, we headed out down a long, paved road into the middle of nowhere. There was a miles-long straightaway in either direction, bordered by pastures and wooded blocks of ranch land, perfect for shining a light and spotting deer.

Usually, an officer would set up in a location in which they could see as far as possible. This meant finding a spot to pull off the shoulder, hiding the car as best he could (either with a surplus army parachute or some cut branches and bushes), and quietly waiting for the light to shine or a shot to ring out.

But this officer had a different plan.

He traveled to a portion of the highway that ended in a blind S-curve. He pulled over under some trees and parked.

"What are we doing here?", I asked. "You can't see any of the road!"

"I've got it all figured out!", he boasted.

He immediately walked over to a tall oak tree and started

climbing up some board steps he had attached to the tree. Before I knew it, he was 30 feet up, sitting on a small wooden platform between two branches.

"I can see for miles in both directions from up here...and they never expect for me to be here! I'm perfectly hidden."

"Well, that's all fine and dandy," I responded, "but how you gonna get down in time to stop anyone? By the time you climb back down in the pitch-black dark and get to your truck, they'll be long gone! That's assuming you don't break your neck on the way down the steps."

"Just watch!"

No sooner than I asked the question, he summoned his inner "Tarzan" and swung down from the platform on a rope he had tied to a higher branch. Just that quick, he was back in his truck ready to go.

"There ain't no way I'm doing that", I told him.

"You don't have to! You ain't the one that's gotta be workin' out here!"

"Point taken", I thought.

We didn't have any action that night, but sure enough, about a week later, he made a fire hunting case from his perch on that very same road.

One of the most valuable traits I looked for in my officers was creativity. The ingenuity needed to come up with his plan made him a valuable asset to the agency. He ended up being

**121**

one of my best officers.

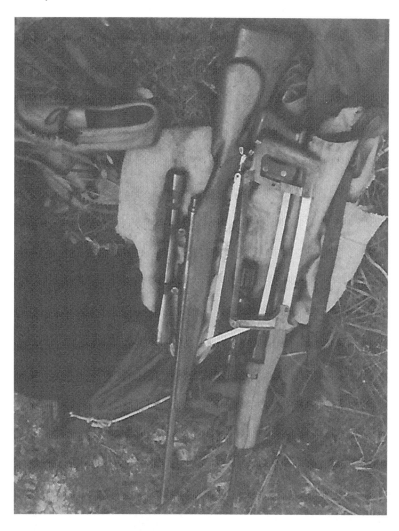

This was evidence taken from an outlaw. The tools of the trade: a gun, a couple saws, and a change of clothes were all a good deer chasing outlaw needed.

## *"Tiger Trainer"*

One of the more gruesome events that took place during my time in Citrus County involved a big cat trainer.

He was well known in the area as the man who trained lions and tigers for the circus. He had several of the big predators housed on his property. As I previously touched on, part of my job was inspecting these facilities and making sure they regulations were being followed and all the safety procedures were in place. I had spoken with him on numerous occasions and had visited the property before. I had never witnessed any problems or violations at the property, as the experienced trainer was normally very careful and professional in his day to day operations.

One day, I received a call that someone had been injured at the big cat facility. So, I made my way to Bevel's Corner, where the property was located. The call for assistance fell short of the horrific scene that I found.

The trainer had been attacked and killed by a large tiger. While attempting to transfer the tiger form one pen to another, one of the doors had not been securely fastened. While the man was moving materials from one pen to another, the large cat attacked him, easily cutting his throat from ear to ear. He quickly bled to death on the ground inside the pen. Unfortunately, his daughter was present at the time and witnessed the entire event. She was understandably hysterical, as her father's body was still inside the pen with the tiger.

After several attempts to get the tiger away from the body, it

**123**

became apparent that the cat would not willingly give up his kill. So, I did what needed to be done and put the animal down.

There have been several stories similar to this one across the state over the years. One of our officers even received anonymous death threats from members of the public after he was forced to shoot a tiger while on duty.

I've always been opposed to keeping big cats in captivity. Large predators are instinctively driven to hunt and kill smaller prey animals. These animals cannot be tamed or trusted in captivity and keeping them in small enclosures only increases the possibility incidents like this one.

## *"The Rainbow River"*

On the northern border of Citrus County lies the Rainbow River. It flows from Rainbow Springs State Park in Dunnellon and connects with the Withlacoochee River, eventually making its way to the Gulf of Mexico.

Because the river is born out of a large flow spring, the water makes its way directly from the lime rock caverns of Florida's underground aquifer system. These springs are some of the best known and most visited, not only in Florida but in the world. Every year, hundreds of thousands of visitors are attracted to the crystal-clear waters which offer a variety of activities, from canoeing and kayaking to fishing and tubing. The water is a constant 72 degrees Fahrenheit, making it perfect for year-round recreational activities.

Because the water is so clear, it also attracts people looking to take advantage of the abundance of fish and wildlife that inhabit the river. One of the biggest problems we faced during my time in Citrus County was illegal spearfishing in the river. Spearfishing in freshwater was, and still is, illegal in Florida.

We would often receive calls from the residents who lived along the river complaining about people spearfishing. As time went on, experience would help us catch many of these poachers. This meant that they would get smarter as well, and harder for us to catch. The more we would arrest them, the better they got at hiding it.

Ingenuity isn't a trait reserved for the good guys.

A perfect example of this occurred one afternoon while I was patrolling the river. I found very early on that patrolling the river by boat was not the best way to catch these people. They recognized the boat from hundreds of yards away and by the time an officer could approach them on the water, they would have dumped any evidence of their misdeeds. They would often keep burlap croaker sacks that they used to store the fish they killed. They would tie the bag to the side of the boat or dangle it from their foot, never taking it out of the water. If an officer approached, they would simply untie the bag allowing it to settle into the grass beds of the river, making it almost impossible to spot from the surface. Even though the water was clear, the brown sacks blended perfectly with the green and brown grass on the bottom.

So, it became my common practice to observe from the shoreline. This offered me a couple of advantages. Since the river was relatively narrow, I could use the trees and structures along the shoreline to stay out of sight. This meant that I could not only observe without being seen, but I could get relatively close without giving away my presence. It also meant that I could avoid potential boat chases which would endanger anyone on the river at the time. There were only a couple of access points for boats along the river and I could reach them in my vehicle fairly quickly.

On this particular day, I had been watching a fella for several hours. He was snorkeling along the river, occasionally diving to the bottom and coming to the surface again. He was clearly handling something under the water and after a while, it became apparent he was carrying a sack and some sort of spear. Once I got as close to him as I felt I could, I walked out onto one of the docks closest to him.

He spotted me immediately.

"Come on over here," I ordered.

By this time, he had already dropped his sack of fish and his spear gun.

"Why? I haven't done anything wrong!"

The man was clearly agitated and began cursing and grumbling. I could see he was deciding whether to fight, flee, or simply give up.

I always found that the best way to approach a situation like this was to first try and reason with the man. Most people, even those breaking the law, responded better to polite reasoning rather than aggression, which would often escalate the situation unnecessarily.

"Listen," I said, "I've been watching you for hours. I already know what you're doing and how you're doing it. At this point, you're under arrest. What happens next is really up to you, but you have two options. Option one is, you can go back and pick up your spear and your sack of fish. All you've done to this point is commit a misdemeanor. The max fine is $500. I'll write you a ticket and you can go on your way. Option two means anything you do besides follow my orders will be considered resisting arrest, which is a felony. That means, you go to jail today, I will take your boat, and you have to bond out on a $5,000 bond. That's going to cost you $500 today. Then you'll have to pay court costs plus whatever else the judge decides. Do you really want to explain to a judge why you resisted arrest over some fish?"

The man thought for a few seconds and then relented.

"Alright", he muttered as he hung his head. He went back into the water and retrieved the evidence of his crimes.

He brought up a sack with several speared bass and a Hawaiian sling. A Hawaiian sling is a sort of homemade spear gun. It consists of a hollow piece of bamboo, a long thin metal rod with a sharpened point, and some surgical tubing used as elastic band to propel the spear. The rod is inserted into the bamboo and propelled by the elastic tubing using only the swimmer's arm and hand. The benefits to using the sling as opposed to a store-bought spear gun were twofold: the sling was homemade and relatively cheap compared to a spear gun, making easily dumped or destroyed if an officer approached. It could also be loaded and fired with one hand, making it easy to use and conceal under the water.

I gathered all the evidence and wrote the ticket. The man wasn't happy, but I'm sure he was glad to avoid the trip to jail and the felony charge.

The crystal-clear waters of Florida's springs draw thousands of visitors every year.

## "Sick Alligators"

A big part of being in law enforcement is knowing that the eyes of the public are always on you. Everything you do and say can be scrutinized, especially in today's world where everyone is a reporter with a microphone and a high-definition camera in their pocket.

Early in my career as a supervisor, I hadn't yet learned that I needed to be extremely careful when talking to the press, especially when it involved highly publicized cases and issues.

One such case involved a large number of alligators in Lake Apopka. Lake Apopka is located near Disney World, just northwest of Orlando. This added to the public nature of the incident, given its close proximity to a very popular tourist destination.

The alligators were mysteriously dying off. We were finding dozens of them in a very short period of time. It became apparent early on that it wasn't poachers. There was no evidence of physical harm to the gators. They were simply dying.

Alligators haven't changed much since the time of the dinosaurs. They are the top predators in Florida's food chain, having no natural predators once they reach maturity. This ruled out any possibility of the gators being killed by a predator.

This meant that something in their environment, whether it was natural or man-made, was making the gators sick. Agency biologists performed multiple necropsy investigations but could not determine what the cause of death was. A team of alligator biologists from Auburn University was called in to investigate further. By that time, the story was all over the news and several press agencies were involved.

It was decided that the best course of action was to attempt to catch a sick gator, one that was still alive and could hopefully offer a clue to the cause of the die-off.

I was sent to the lake to assist the biologists that were there. Since most of the areas supervisors were out in the field or busy elsewhere, I arrived to find myself the only contact between the press and the agency. They asked if I could give a quick interview and answer just a few questions about the situation.

I confidently accepted, eager to show my expertise and to serve as a representative of the commission.

They asked for a brief synopsis of the situation and how we were handling it. I explained our efforts to catch a live gator and detailed how we would go about doing it.

"But how do you know which gators are sick and which ones aren't?"

"Well," I instantly replied, "you can pretty much tell by the expression on his face."

Of course, I was joking. However, the reporter didn't know this. The next day, the quote was in the Orlando Sentinel paper and distributed to all of central Florida.

**131**

For quite some time after that, I was known as the "Sick Alligator Warden". My fellow officers found a great deal of pleasure in reminding me of that.

None of us are perfect. It took me years to live that one down.

It turned out, the gators were falling victim to a strain of botulism. However, the toxin wasn't in the water. The gators were ingesting dead or dying turtles. Eventually, the toxin would build up enough in their system to kill them. This is apparently a very rare occurrence, and this was the first documented instance of such an event.

Towards the end of my career, I started several programs that became very effective in helping organize community members to help various conservation causes around the state.

One of the more successful programs was known as "MOPS", or "Manatee Observation Patrols". It was started in cooperation with the Save the Manatee Club. At the time, the club had more than 43,000 members around the state.

One of the main causes of death and danger for the manatees was impacts with boats. The manatees migrate throughout the rivers and springs of Florida, looking for food and warm-water shelter from the winter weather. Since the springs of Florida maintain a relatively warm temperature year-round, this brings the manatees into close contact with boaters travelling those same waterways.

The manatees that travel the St. Johns River are especially vulnerable. The water in the river is very dark and the manatees are especially difficult to see. In those days, it was rare to find an adult manatee that did not have cuts or scars along its back from being struck by a boat propeller. It was one of our top priorities with the agency to protect the then endangered species.

In cooperation with the department of transportation, I placed temperature sensors at the three main bridges along the St. Johns and monitored them closely, knowing that once the water reached a certain temperature, the manatees would

**133**

begin to migrate in large groups up and down the waterway.

MOPS enlisted the help of hundreds of volunteers who would locate and track the large groups of slow moving marine mammals, and follow them closely in their personal boats, making other boaters aware of their presence. It was not uncommon to see groups of 30 or 40 manatees moving together along the river.

It was also part of our job to issue citations to boaters who did not observe the slow speed manatee zones posted around the state.

As a result of these and other efforts across the whole state of Florida, the manatees' numbers have grown and even though they are still protected, they are no longer listed as an endangered species. Over the past decade, manatee deaths from boat strikes have dropped dramatically.

Today, the manatees are one of the most (if not the most) popular tourist attractions for eco-tourism in the state. Manatee sight-seeing generates millions of dollars for the communities that harbor them and the businesses that operate there.

I am extremely grateful to the countless volunteers, employees, and political figures who helped make the manatee's story a successful one. With their numbers at record highs, I'm confident the manatees will be around for generations to come.

Mating groups of
manatees migrate up and
down the St. Johns River.

I received an award for my work with the MOPS.

## *"Dove Hunting"*

As a lifelong hunter and fisherman, I enjoyed taking a part in many of the activities that I was responsible for monitoring on a day to day basis as a game warden. One of the activities that I really enjoyed was dove hunting.

Doves are small migratory birds that typically travel in large flocks. They will focus on areas with large concentrations of food. Often, this means you can find them in heavy numbers around farmlands and agricultural fields. Since they congregate in these places, hunters will organize a "dove shoot". Several hunters or groups of hunters will scatter themselves around a field and hide in the brush around the edge of the field, or near hay bales or other artificial cover placed in the field itself. Since the doves feed mostly on grain and seeds, they are prized as a source of food by many hunters. Not to mention, they are a great challenge to shoot. They are fast flyers and rapidly change direction and speed in the air.

When the birds come in to feed in the field, the hunters are able to ambush the birds, often killing hundreds of them in a single afternoon. Even given the high numbers that are harvested, and even though only ten percent of them live more than one year because of natural causes, the dove populations remain healthy.

The birds are hunted with shotguns loaded with birdshot. In most places, the law states that the birds can only be shot from sun up to sun down, and hunters must keep their shotgun magazines "plugged". This means that a small plastic or wooden dowel is inserted in the magazine to prevent the

**137**

gun from holding more than three shells. Typical violations in a dove field ranged from hunters taking too many birds (over the legal limit, which was 12 birds) to hunters removing the plugs from their shotguns and firing too many shots. It's also very tempting for hunters to continue shooting after the sun sets. This is the time right before dark that the birds seek a watering hole before going to roost. This makes them vulnerable to over-harvesting, as well as making it difficult for hunters to retrieve the birds in the dark, meaning many birds were lost and wasted.

Later in the dove season, as the food supplies dwindled, it became more and more common for outlaw hunters to "bait" the birds, adding grains like cracked corn or millet seed to a field in order to attract more birds. This is also considered unsportsmanlike and is illegal.

As a bird hunter myself, I understood the temptations involved and for these reasons, as I got older, I gave up dove hunting.

When I initially arrived as a first-time supervisor, the strategy employed by most officers was simple: drive your patrol car into an active field and check everyone. The problem with this strategy is it gives violators time to conceal their violations and replace their shotgun plugs or dispose of extra harvested birds. As a result, very few dove cases were being made. The hunters always saw us coming.

So, I decided to train my officers in a different technique. We would meet up and park away from the field, out of sight from any hunters. Then, we could approach on foot with a pair of binoculars and wait. Giving ourselves time to observe was vital.

Many hunters would kill their birds and hide them away from where they were shooting. They did this to avoid being caught with too many birds on them. When the coast was clear, they simply retrieved the birds and went on their way.

If we watched the hunters for some time before approaching, we would already know who was stashing their birds where, as well as who was firing too many shots at a time. This became a very productive method of working dove hunters. Not long after we employed these tactics, the word spread among the hunters that we were out in force, and violations slowed significantly. This quickly became the preferred method for all officers to patrol dove fields. Strategies like these protect the precious resources of our state from over-harvesting and criminal activity. To many poachers, it's a game. To win the game, you need to be smarter than your opponent and have a little patience.

Bird-hunting is a popular
sport in Florida. Here, we
are identifying birds taken
by hunters.

140

### "Traveling Fish Saleswoman"

As a lieutenant, one of the more memorable cases I worked involved a well-known commercial fisherman near Sanford. I had received a tip that he was catching large numbers of specks (crappie) and selling them up north somewhere. I tried for several weeks to catch him in the act, but he was extremely careful and I often didn't find out about his catches until after the fact. I knew he wasn't transporting the fish up the river, so he must have been offloading them into a truck somewhere. As hard as I tried, I could never find that truck. So, I started keeping an eye on when he was home and when he was out fishing, and I asked our investigators to help out.

One night, we got lucky and happened to notice he was out. I went by his house and his boat and truck were gone. After looking for a short while, I spotted him on the river. I followed him from land as best I could, but lost sight of him near the shoreline across the river, in an area I knew could be accessed from the road. Figuring he must be dropping the fish to a driver with a truck, I headed that way as fast as I could.

I was almost there when I saw something I didn't expect. I saw his wife's car heading out as I was heading in. It took a moment for me to realize who I had just seen, and that she had surely seen me. I also realized at that moment, I shouldn't have been looking for a truck.

I slammed on the brakes and spun around. She had a pretty good head start and as far as I could tell, she was standing on the gas pedal. I give her credit for being an excellent driver. I followed her for several miles, just catching glimpses of her tail lights as she would brake to corner. I never managed to get closer than about a quarter mile. Eventually, incorrectly assuming I knew where she was headed, I made a wrong turn and I lost her. I got on the radio, but there was no sign of her anywhere. I knew I had one last chance to catch her and it was a desperate longshot.

I called to our regional office in Lake City, more than 2 hours to the north. We knew she was heading to Georgia and there were only a few main routes she could take. Still, she had the entire width of the state to travel, and I had only a few sets of eyes working at the time. I put out a BOLO and hoped for the best. Dejected, I turned around and headed home.

A couple hours or so went by without a word from up north. I was convinced she had escaped. I was already settled in for the night when the phone began to ring around 4 a.m. It was Officer Woodall out of Lake City. He had spotted her heading up Interstate 75 and managed to stop her. He took her into custody and towed the car and fish to the office. I immediately headed to our Lake City office.

What I found when I got there was incredible.

The man and his wife had removed the back seat from her car and lined the trunk and the interior with a tarp. Inside the car was over 500 pounds of specks. They had devised an almost perfect plan. No one would ever suspect the sedan to be filled with illegal fish. Had I not recognized the car as his wife's, I would never have given it a second glance. To this day, it remains one of the most interesting cases I was ever involved in.

The entire trunk and back seat were filled with fish.

As her husband was sitting back home down south, the dejected woman stood by as we emptied hundreds of pounds of illegally harvested fish from the trunk and back seat of her car. If not for the quick work of a very observant officer, Ofc. Woodall, in Lake City, she would have escaped.

### *"Flying to My Death"*

I never enjoyed flying in the Commission's aircraft. It wasn't that I was afraid to fly. Having been in the Air Force and having flown around the world a couple times, I wasn't bothered by flying.

What worried me was landing in some of the rural areas and unlit runways that we used.

Often times, the best way to patrol for fire hunters at night was to fly over an area and look for the shine of a spotlight in the vast midnight darkness of the Florida wilderness. Usually, this meant landing in some pretty sketchy areas to refuel or meet up with officers on the ground. Some of the places we landed were damn near invisible in the best weather. Many times, in the early morning hours when the dewpoint is reached causing fog to roll in, seeing the runway became impossible.

I will never forget the sound of the stall alarm on that small, single-engine aircraft. Our pilots were excellent, but when the hum of the engine on approach is interrupted by the most God-awful buzzer you've ever heard, parts of you pucker up in a hurry. It's an eerie feeling knowing the ground is fast approaching and not being able to see it.

I'm reminded of a joke I heard a comedian tell once:

A man asks the pilot, "If the engine dies, how far can we go?"

The pilot replies, "All the way to the scene of the crash."

## 145

We made many fire hunting cases from the seat of an airplane. Seeing that spotlight from high above always got my heart pumping a little bit faster. I imagine sailors in the days before electronics and GPS must have felt similar seeing that lighthouse on the dark distant horizon. Those aircraft remain an invaluable tool to this day, but they are one part of the job I don't miss. Our pilots were some of the most skilled I have ever seen, and they were some of the best officers I had ever known.

Throughout Florida, many of the best hunting areas and WMA's are bordered by military bases and bombing ranges. Many of the poachers assumed that we could not fly our airplane in these restricted areas, so they became choice areas for criminal poaching activity. Sometimes this meant that we would fly our aircraft near or in airspace used by military aircraft during their exercises. We would file our flight plan with the correct military authorities so they would know where we were and hopefully avoid us.

One night, while working fire hunters near a large forest, we ended up near the Naval bombing range in that area. We had filed the flight plan through the proper channels, but somewhere along the line, there was a miscommunication.

We were flying without our navigation lights to remain unseen from the ground. This also meant we were unseen in the air. Halfway through our flight, we were buzzed by a jet, easily doing 600 to 700 mph. The jet must have passed within only a few hundred feet and our small plane flew through the jet wash. When this happened, our plane nearly flipped upside down. Thankfully, my pilot was able to recover quickly or we likely would have crashed in the middle of nowhere.

Again, major pucker factor.

I also disliked flying during the day. We often used the plane to operate search and rescue missions for missing boaters or fisherman, or for hunters lost in the woods. As the hot Florida sun heats the surface of the land, it creates severe updrafts. These are responsible for creating the afternoon storms our state is so famous for. It also makes flying in a small aircraft akin to being on a 45-minute roller coaster ride. The constant bouncing and turning created by the changing air patterns was like floating on the ocean during a squall.  I'm proud to say I never threw up, but on more than one occasion, I was completely worthless in the passenger seat of that plane. Battling motion sickness was not my favorite way to spend a day on the job.

This was also one of the reasons I sought out my next promotion. Along with more responsibility, a bigger area, and more officers to work with, the thought of being able to assign someone else to ride shotgun in the plane brought a great relief to my mind. I would occasionally still fly (in the best weather on the clearest moonlit nights) just so my officers wouldn't think I was a wussy.

My next promotion allowed my family and I to finally move out of our mobile trailer home and into a small house on a piece of land in Ft. McCoy. The size of the area I became responsible for grew exponentially. My area became a large triangle from St. Augustine all the way down to Cape Canaveral, all the way back over to Marion County.

The small Cessna 172
helped us make many fire
hunting cases, but it could
be a rough ride at times.

## *"Another New Area...New Adventures"*

With my new promotion to lieutenant, I gained some of the most popular hunting and fishing areas in the state. These included the Ocala National Forest, Lake George, and most of the St. Johns River. I also gained a larger crew, including 4 or 5 sergeants and approximately 25 officers.

The Ocala National Forest is popular with hunters, fishermen, and tourists alike. This nearly 400,000-acre wilderness offers many activities and natural resources for anyone seeking to enjoy the outdoors. It is also a very popular area for fire hunting, with countless clear-cut timber areas and roads cut through the forest.

The St. Johns River, which flows into and out of Lake George, is a very popular commercial fishery. Because it flows north to the Atlantic Ocean, the river contains an abundance of both freshwater and saltwater species. Along with the recreational sport fishing resources, the river holds many commercial fisheries including blue crabs, shrimp, and catfish. These were harvested in a variety of ways, including traps, gill nets, cast nets, seins, and even an illegal tactic known as "monkey fishing", in which the fish are electrocuted in the water.

All of this meant I would be extremely busy from day to day. It also meant my men would stay busy, making my job as their supervisor even more important. I was responsible for reviewing the reports on the cases filed by my officers, making sure they were accurate and met the standard necessary to hold up in a court of law. Many of the stories that follow are the accounts of such cases. I wanted to make sure and give

**149**

credit to those officers for their hard work and accomplishments.

I am seated in the front center, with a group of officers and sergeants that I supervised as a lieutenant. Also pictured are my captain and regional commander, as well our regional secretary, Joyce.

**LT. WAYNE KING**

Lt. Wayne King, Wildlife Officer and area supervisor for law enforcement for six counties including Marion, was questioned recently about activities of the Florida Game and Fresh Water Fish Commission.

**QUESTION**—What does a Wildlife Officer do in his work?

**ANSWER**—Functions vary from what was done in the past. The job comprises many aspects of law enforcement and related duties. It ranges from arresting a poacher at night using a gunning light to assisting in riot control duty in various parts of the state. We are also called on to assist, and also to lead, search and rescue missions. We also assist in the time of any natural disaster, such as hurricanes, as we are familiar with the country.

**QUESTION**—Then you do not only enforce game and fish laws, but others as well?

**ANSWER**—Our primary effort is to enforce the game and fish laws, but we have been given full law enforcement powers and responsibilities.

**QUESTION**—Why do Wildlife Officers carry guns?

**ANSWER**—For defense of the officer's life. In the last two years, four officers have been shot enforcing the game and fish laws. Two of these were killed.

**QUESTION**—Are the game and fish laws misdemeanors or felonies?

**ANSWER**—Most are misdemeanors, but a few, such as the alligator law, are felonies. The alligator law means that attempting to take, kill, molest or possess an alligator is a felony.

**QUESTION**—What court handles your game and fish laws?

**ANSWER**—The County Courts. The commission greatly appreciates the support the courts have shown to the game and fish department in Marion County. Marion is fortunate to have the type of judges that it does.

**QUESTION**—What are normal working hours for a Wildlife Officer?

**ANSWER**—We work day and night. An officer is generally assigned to one county, but can be assigned anywhere in the state. His hours vary depending on the demands of any job at the time. He could leave home and be gone three or four days, camping out, trying to catch an illegal fish device, or possibly on a search or rescue mission that may keep him going 48 or 60 hours straight.

**QUESTION**—Do you have any reserve group, or other supporters?

**ANSWER**—We have a reserve group that has just been started. Interested persons may contact the local office in Ocala for information. There is no pay, and the reserve must furnish his own uniform and insurance. He must pass a written and oral examination.

We also have excellent help through an outstanding search and rescue unit. The people of Marion County are fortunate to have such an outstanding unit under Sheriff Don Moreland. They have been a great asset to the people of Marion County.

**QUESTION**—What is the attitude of the people of Marion County toward game and fish law enforcement?

**ANSWER**—The attitude is very good. We have received tremendous support from the public, and it has been greatly appreciated. We could not do the job half as good without the eyes and ears of the public. We could accomplish very little without the conscientious persons who frown on the man who is bragging about his over limit or his doe deer.

Most people understand that our fish and game belong to everyone, and resent any individual who breaks the law.

## "The Value of a Good Officer"

I was very fortunate in my time as a lieutenant, and later as a captain, in this part of the state. It's where I spent the remainder of my career and it's where I was able to accomplish the things I am most proud of when I look back on it. The main reason for this was my officers, sergeants, and lieutenants.

These men and women could have been anything they chose to be. They were some of the most well-educated, talented, intelligent, and successful people that I had ever had the pleasure of meeting. But they each chose to answer the call of the wild, and took up the mantle of game warden. They were all quick learners, which made teaching them more enjoyable and trusting them much easier. I knew I could rely on them and that I didn't have to spend my time micromanaging their every move. An important part of being an effective supervisor is developing a good team. The ones who couldn't cut it usually moved on quickly, or were moved along with my help, when I felt it was necessary.

This gave me the freedom to pursue many of my goals in this new position. I wanted to improve public relations with the agency, increase efficiency, and cut operating costs. These things would go a long way toward enhancing the image of the agency, providing more career enhancement opportunities for our officers, and towards serving the public and wildlife better.

As a captain, I was privileged to have some of the best officers and lieutenants in the state.

### "Too Good to Be True"

In all my years as a supervisor, I only had 2 officers (out of about a hundred) that never received a single complaint filed against them. When you consider that no one likes to be arrested or receive a ticket, even if deep down they know they deserve it, you understand how amazing it is that those officers never had a complaint lodged against them. This is not to say that other officers who had complaints filed on them were not good officers, because they certainly were. It's just remarkable to think that you could do this job for years on end and never tick off someone enough to make them pick up a phone and call your boss.

One of those officers was Al Clifton. Al has since passed away, but he worked for me in Volusia county for more than 25 years. He could have been promoted many times, but Al liked where he was and what he was doing. The people in Al's area always referred to him as "Mr. Clifton". This told me that everyone had a great deal of respect for Al. I suspect it had a great deal to do with his disposition.

One day, I was working with Al and we decided to take a break for lunch. We had packed our lunches and figured we would stop under an oak hammock to eat in the shade. Al was another example of an officer who liked everything nice and neat. He pulled out his sandwich, wrapped neatly in wax paper. I remember vividly watching him carefully unwrap the sandwich without tearing the paper. Right as he was about to take a bite, a bird in the tree above him pooped, giving Al a nice little topping in the dead center of his sandwich. Al didn't even flinch. He didn't curse or get angry. He looked up at the bird, then looked to me.

"You know, they just sing for most people."

I suspect that calm demeanor and positive outlook is why no one ever had a bad word to say about Al.

Back then, the Game Commission was very frugal in their purchases of equipment. Al had an old Critchfield patrol boat. He had that boat for the better part of 15 years and had taken great care of it. He had spent his own money to put a windshield on the boat when the state wouldn't buy him one.

Eventually, I got Al a new boat, which of course he didn't want. I wanted to give Al's old boat to another officer who didn't have one. This particular officer was stubborn and didn't want to patrol on the water. I forced that officer to take Al's boat and spend time on the water. Oddly enough, the first thing he did was remove the windshield. Go figure.

The other officer I never received a complaint on was Hugh "Danton" Jones. He worked for me in Marion County for 25 years. Whenever we would have trainings or meetings, I would use those opportunities to create scenarios for my officers to show them what to do and what not to do in certain situations. I always liked to use Danton and Al as teachers by having them demonstrate how they dealt with the people they interacted with in the woods and on the water. I never wanted to embarrass either of them, so when they weren't around, I would tell my other officers that the reason they never got any complaints against them was because of how they treated the

**155**

public. I encouraged my other officers to think about what they saw demonstrated that day. Al and Danton served as great examples of how to uphold the standards of professionalism I expected from our officers.

## *"Designated Boaters"*

One of the most attractive things about this part of the state is the accessibility of its waterways. There are hundreds of spring-fed lakes and rivers in the area. These are very popular with boaters, especially on holiday weekends in the spring and summer months. It is not uncommon to see hundreds, even thousands, of boaters congregate in and around the clearwater springs scattered throughout our state. These high traffic areas can become dangerous when combined with large amounts of alcohol sometimes consumed by boat operators.

It was especially problematic because the majority of the public simply wasn't aware that "driving under the influence" laws applied to boats in the same way they applied to cars on the highway. There is a legal blood alcohol limit for the operator of a vessel just as there is for the driver of a car. The charge is "boating under the influence" or "BUI". When coupled with the hot Florida sun, consuming alcoholic beverages can have a more profound impact on the driver of a boat.

This led to many boating accidents that resulted in extensive property damage, severe personal injury, and occasionally the death of a boater.

In order to both educate the public and cut down on these unfortunate events, I sought out the help of a group of activists, MADD, or Mothers Against Drunk Drivers. They had been successful in running a campaign to cut down on incidents of drunk driving on the roadways of the state.

Together, we lobbied businesses to develop a program for designated operators, offering incentives like free meals or other rewards, to ensure that a sober designated driver was operating a boat during these busy holiday weekends. Drivers were given bracelets to wear, identifying them as the designated boater, and businesses along the river would offer the incentives. This not only created revenues for these businesses but helped keep every boater safer on the water. It also helped our officers be more effective and improved our image in the eyes of the public. My area received a nationally recognized award from MADD because of this program. The publicity associated with the award and the program helped educate countless boaters, ultimately saving lives and cutting down on boating accidents in my area.

I was also very proud of the number of successful BUI cases my officers made during my time as a supervisor. We put a great deal of work into making these cases and refining the techniques we used to enforce BUI laws. Making a BUI cases is one of the more difficult tasks an officer can undertake.

Consider this: When a State Trooper or Sheriff's Deputy makes a DUI stop, they have already witnessed the vehicle swerving over the yellow line or driving erratically. They get the driver out of the vehicle, on solid ground, and have the driver perform a set of sobriety tasks, many of which require the driver to walk a straight line, stand on one leg, or tilt their head back with their eyes closed. They use all of this as evidence to support their case against the drunk driver.

Now imagine having to do all of this on the water, in a boat, where factors like wind, tidal current, and boat wake can make it difficult for even the soberest of people to stand on two legs, let alone one leg. How do you make a suspected drunk boater walk a straight line? I have tried to draw a perfectly straight line on the surface of the water, many times in fact. If you ever figure out how, look me up. I'd love to know.

Usually, stopping a suspected drunk boater meant finding a place on the hill to have them perform the sobriety tasks. Parking lots at boat ramps often had painted lines that were perfect for this, but what if you were miles from the nearest boat ramp?

In a pinch, a dock or pier could be used. But what if the boater was barefoot? Could you ask a barefoot boater to walk a straight line on a shell island or a hot parking lot? If the boater was alone, how did you transport him to jail while simultaneously ensuring that his boat didn't drift off or sink? What do you do to get a boat several miles from where you stopped it to the shore, so you can perform the tests on the driver? Do you let the driver drive the boat, potentially crashing while under your supervision? Do you get another officer to drive the boat, opening the agency up to liability for damage to the boat that may already be there? These problems were unique to working BUI's. Our officers needed to improvise as best they could to ensure the case was solid and that they weren't taking innocent people to jail. I'm proud to say that as far as I can remember, we never lost a BUI case in court. My officers were well-trained and worked hard to make sure they were keeping boaters safe and holding law breakers accountable.

**159**

My officers played a great role in making the waterways a safer place to be.

## *"Diversity in the Agency"*

One of the most important things I wanted to focus on as a supervisor was creating diversity within the agency, specifically within the division of law enforcement. Traditionally, all our officers were white males. Even though the population of Florida had always been a culturally diverse group, our agency did not always reflect this same diversity. I believed that doing so would improve the public image of the agency and make interacting with the public easier and safer for all our officers.

I approached the head honchos in Tallahassee with the idea, and they were all for it. I suggested we create minority recruiters in all our regional offices. I volunteered to become a recruiter, and served as an agency contact at several of the state's traditionally black colleges. This effort helped us find, recruit, and hire minorities and provided a much-needed public relations boost with our customers.

It wasn't until in the late 70's and early 80's that the push to hire women gave us our first female officers. One initial roadblock to hiring women came in the form of our chosen sidearm. At the time, we all carried .357 magnum revolvers. The guns were large and bulky, and made it difficult for female recruits to pass the training certification. Typically, women tended to have smaller hands and this simply made accurate shooting with the revolver more difficult. It wasn't that the women couldn't shoot, but more that the weapon we were asking them to use was a physical impediment to their abilities.

So, it was during this time that the agency decided to move to

**161**

the smaller frame of a semi-automatic Colt. Initially, I was opposed to the change, until I realized how much easier the Colt was to shoot and how many more rounds we could carry. The revolver held only 6 shots and was slow to reload. The new semi-autos held 14 rounds and were easily reloaded by switching out the magazines. This meant that an officer carrying 2 extra magazines could potentially have around 40 rounds at their disposal.

If I remember correctly, at one point I had the second and third female officers to ever be hired by the agency working in my area. Given their smaller stature, I was worried at first. This job can be extremely demanding physically, and I often worried for their safety, especially in the remote locations we spent most of our time working alone. However, I also realized that they brought new ideas and perspectives to the team and these would prove invaluable throughout my career.

One of these female officers was Janice Jones. Janice worked most of her career for me in Flagler, Marion, and the surrounding areas. Since I was one of the people pushing for these new hires, I wanted to make sure she got a good start with the agency.

I always tried to push my officers to come up with new ideas to help us do our jobs. I was riding with one of my lieutenants at the time and asked him about how Janice was doing.

"She's doing fine. She's making a map of the area and putting together a contact list of land owners."

The idea was to create a map of the local ranches and

properties, so that if we needed to get into a locked gate or an area we couldn't easily access, we would know immediately who to contact. It was an impressive idea and would make getting around easier for all of us.

I wanted to see the map, so we called Janice and set up a meeting. Apparently, I had failed to properly train this lieutenant, as we met on the side of the road, in full view of the blazing summer sun.

"Next time I ask for a meeting, pick a shady spot."

So, Janice pulled out her map and sprawled it across the hood of her patrol car. I was blown away by the detail and effort she had put into making the map. It even had a legend, as any good map should, that described different locations and symbols on the map.

I congratulated Janice and told her she was doing a great job. I asked her to keep up the good work.

I should have ended the meeting with that. However, without much thought, I added that it was nice to have a female game warden because they definitely smelled better than the male ones.

I meant nothing by it and was attempting to make a joke. I found out later that I had offended Janice and that she considered my remark inappropriate. I later apologized and even though I already knew that I needed to be careful with how I spoke around female officers, in this case I had slipped up.

Janice and I became very good friends and she was one of the best officers I ever worked with. We remain close friends to this day.

One of my favorite stories involving Janice happened on a holiday weekend at Silver Glen Springs, on the southwest side of Lake George. Silver Glen is one of those places that are extremely popular with boaters in the summer. The glen has a short run that empties into Lake George and it fills with boats on hot weekends. Sometimes, hundreds of boats will pack in to the glen, often rafting together in a tight group. At times, it was possible to walk from boat to boat and check them all without ever touching the water. It was essentially one big floating party.

I had access to a private piece of land that butts up to the glen. On busy weekends, we used this spot as a base of operations. We could even land the agency helicopter if the need arose.

On this day, I was standing on the shore watching over the run, when I saw a boat attempting to flee from one of our patrol vessels. It was Janice and it turned out the man attempting to flee was a drunk driver. He ran his boat up into the bushes and hopped out, attempting to run up into the park. I guessed he had about a hundred-yard head start on Janice.

Well, Janice was having none of it. She ran her boat up the run at about 25 miles per hour in pursuit of the fleeing drunk boater. She grounded the patrol boat right up onto the shore and I remember seeing her fly through the air as she jumped out of the boat, into the swamp, and took off after the man. A couple minutes later, she had run him down, handcuffed him, and brought him back. This was just one of many dangerous situations that she was involved in and I learned very early on that she could be trusted with any job. For this reason, she was one of the people I always chose to assist with specific operations and details we performed.

Me, with Ofc. Janice Jones in costume, during patrol on Halloween.

## "My Next Promotion"

It wasn't long after I moved to Marion county that the agency had a supervisory reorganization. My position at that time was as a lieutenant. This meant I was supervising a crew of sergeants, who in turn were each responsible for supervising a crew of officers. To better align with other state agencies' supervisory structures, some of our sergeants became investigators and moved to their own division within law enforcement. This meant that lieutenants became directly responsible for the officer crews. This meant that I was now a captain. The promotion was based more on the restructuring and my duties remained essentially the same. I would retain this rank for the remainder of my career. To this day, most people I meet when I'm out and about call me "Captain King".

As a captain, I was well known for spending a great deal of my time in the field with my officers. Many of my counterparts relished the captain's position because it allowed them to spend more time in the office, in the air conditioning, and attending meetings and lunches. I really felt that to be sure my officers and lieutenants had everything they needed and to make sure I was aware of how things were going in the field, I needed to be in the field as much as possible. For the most part, I was only in the office one day a week. This was necessary to perform all the administrative tasks, like filing reports and signing purchasing orders. The rest of my time was spent patrolling with my officers, sergeants, and lieutenants.

I also made a point of educating our judges, district attorneys, and prosecutors as to the methods and dangers of the job we

**167**

were doing. I would often invite them on flights with the agency or on a ride-along with my officers and lieutenants. This helped them understand how we operated and made it easier to prosecute cases in the courts. The laws we enforced were sometimes obscure and well-known only to our officers and the criminals they pursued. Understanding these laws and the violations associated with them was vital to making sure that a prosecutor or judge could understand the cases we presented to the courts.

### "Monkey Fishing Maniac"

I had an officer working for me in Putnam County who had a unique way of working boaters and fishermen in the St. Johns River. He would sit on top of the bridge in Palatka that crosses over the river and watch from high above. From his perch over the water, he could use his binoculars to see inside of any boat within sight of the bridge.

One day, he caught sight of a notorious monkey fisherman headed towards the bridge.

Monkey fishing was a very popular way for poachers to harvest a large number of catfish in a very short period. Monkey fishing was so named for the contraption that was used to stun the fish. The fishermen would use a machine much like an old-style telephone, which created an electrical charge when the handle was cranked. Two separate wires attached to the machine were lowered on each side of the boat and the electrical current traveled between them. Using the machine resembled an old-time organ grinder with a dancing monkey. The fish in the water would be stunned and float belly up. Catfish were especially susceptible to this method of fishing because of their whiskers, or "barbels" as they are known. Once the fish were floating, they could easily be dipped up in a net. A monkey fisherman could harvest hundreds of pounds of fish in a matter of minutes.

Usually, the monkey fishermen would never return to the boat ramp or travel around the river with the machine on the boat. They knew that merely possessing the machine while fishing was illegal, so they would stash it along the shoreline until they were sure the coast was clear, retrieve it, shock the fish, then replace the hidden machine. So, catching a monkey fisherman in the act or with the illegal gear on the boat was essential to making the case.

As the fisherman approached the bridge, the officer realized two very important things:

The boat was filled with catfish and, more importantly, the fisherman still had his monkey machine on board. Faced with only a few seconds to make a decision, he made a choice that I probably would not have made.

He was a good 10 feet above the water on the bridge. Knowing that if he called out to the man in the boat, the driver would simply flee, the officer decided the best course of action was to jump. It would certainly provide the element of surprise and eliminate the possibility of escape for the poacher.

As the boat travelled beneath him, he let loose of the bridge. Picture a moving boat, no wider than a man laying down, filled with fish and bobbing in the current of the river. The falling officer landed squarely in the vessel, right in the middle of a pile of slimy and spiny catfish.

Needless to say, there wasn't much to discuss after that. The case was open and shut. He made the arrest, seized the boat, fish, and monkey machine, and had one hell of a story to tell everyone.

It was sometime later that I asked him about his decision to jump. Although I was impressed with the result, as his supervisor I had some concerns. What if he had missed? What if he had hurt himself? Worse still, what if he had landed on the fisherman and hurt or killed him?

"Well, I never gave it much thought," he told me.

As a supervisor, it was always my job to consider the worst possibility and prepare my officers as best I could. Don't get me wrong, I was extremely happy with how the case worked out, but I always did my best to help my officers consider how their daily decisions could impact everyone they encountered. At the end of the day, everyone needed to go home safely, officer and poacher alike.

While not the recommended way of catching outlaw fishermen, it was certainly effective.

## "Fainting Fisherwoman"

I spent a great deal of time traveling around my area and visiting my crews. This often meant long days and late nights spent driving over a fifth of the state. Late one night (or early one morning to be accurate), I was on my way back to Ocala from St. Augustine when I came up behind a vehicle towing a skipjack, a long skinny boat popular with commercial fishermen. I had my windows down and could smell the strong fish odor coming from the boat and could see the water dripping from the back and hitting my windshield. It was around 3 a.m. and I suspected that I had happened upon a commercial fisherman, potentially a monkey fisherman, heading home with a boat load of fish and possibly even a monkey machine onboard. I suspected there would be at least one violation and having seen enough evidence of his fishing activities, I decided to stop him.

I turned on my blue light as we approached the barge canal bridge south of Palatka. The bridge that crosses the river there is extremely tall and there is a very steep embankment off the shoulder on the run up to the top of the bridge. The driver pulled over to the shoulder about three-quarters of the way up the overpass. As I walked up to the side of the vehicle, I saw a man and his wife, and a young child sleeping on the front seat. There were no fish in the boat but there was still plenty of slime and water left in the bottom of the vessel. I was convinced that they had been monkey fishing and that there could be a monkey machine in the vehicle, so I decided to get the adults out of the car and look inside.

**173**

The driver was standing at the front of the vehicle and the woman was leaning on the guard rail next to the passenger side of the vehicle. Their child was still asleep on the seat. I looked under the passenger seat and found a small bag of marijuana.

It's important to remember that this was happening more than 30 years ago when that sort of drug violation was a very serious offense. I searched the rest of the vehicle and found no other issues.

The man and the woman were convinced they were in deep trouble. I had not yet decided how to handle the situation when I looked over at the mother just in time to see her faint. She fell backwards over the guard rail and proceeded to tumble down the embankment like a lifeless ragdoll.

Her husband and I took off after her down the hill, keeping a flashlight beam on her as she tumbled for what seemed like forever. I was certain we would find her severely injured if not dead when we finally reached her.

Miraculously, when we got to her, she was awake and unharmed. She cartwheeled down more than a hundred feet of embankment and barely had a scratch on her. We were all three a bit shaken as we made our way back up the hill to the sleeping child.

Feeling like they had been through enough, I decided to offer them a compromise.

"You both know how serious this is, and if I arrest you, your kid is gonna have two parents in jail and have to deal with state child services. So, we're just gonna destroy this right now."

I crumpled up the joints and threw them out.

"Now, I don't expect any trouble out of you in the future and if I ever need your help with anything, I expect you'll be cooperative."

They gratefully agreed and we parted ways. It was only a few weeks later when I received a call from the same man offering me some very specific information on a well-known monkey fisherman who was also using a gill net to catch fish in the river. My crew easily made that net case and shut down the poacher's activity.

This was a common occurrence and I received a great deal of confidential information over the years by cutting breaks when I could. Commercial fishermen were notoriously territorial and would turn each other in when they felt infringed upon by one another. It was not uncommon for them to get into altercations and on occasion even attempt to seriously harm or kill one another.

## "Attending Your Own Funeral"

One of the best officers I ever had working for me was Mike Thomas. Mike had a knack for making great cases and chasing down law breakers. He had worked for me as a reservist during my time in Citrus County. Reservists did not get paid and worked strictly as volunteers. They also had to purchase all their own gear. For this reason, they received special consideration in the hiring process when positions became available. Mike gave up a good paying career as an engineer to become a game warden. He came to work for me in Volusia County and lived in New Smyrna Beach. He worked for me his entire career as an officer.

As with all of the coastal counties in Florida, Volusia had a number of very wealthy and influential people living there. Many of them, despite their affluence, were still skilled poachers and law breakers.

Mike once made an illegal deer hunting case on a well-known business owner in Volusia County. In the course of the arrest, the man told Mike that one day he was gonna kill him. Statements like that were not uncommon in those days and Mike didn't think much of it at the time. It turned out to be a bit more serious than we initially thought.

The man Mike arrested had plenty of money, and he was determined to use it against Mike. The man actually bought a used hearse and had a coffin made to put in the back. He painted the letters "MT" with a big "X" on the coffin and drove the hearse around Volusia, telling everyone he was gonna kill Mike and put him in that coffin. He also had one of his employees drive the hearse around while on the job.

Needless to say, this got a lot of attention. Ultimately, I had to reassign Mike for a short period while we investigated the man for threatening a law enforcement officer. We ended up making other poaching cases against the man and he eventually made himself scarce. After the hearse and coffin incident, he was on the radar of every officer we had. It became difficult for him to do much hunting or fishing after that. It was obvious he wanted attention and we were more than happy to give him ours. My officers were like a family and if you messed with one of them, you messed with all of them. Ultimately, justice served itself, as the man died before his trial.

There are many wilderness areas around the state that are open year-round and are popular with all kinds of recreational users in addition to hunters. The Ocala National Forest is frequently used by hikers, horseback riders, campers, and bird watchers. So, at any time throughout the year, the forest is filled with people enjoying nature and all our state's wilderness areas have to offer.

It also is a popular area for criminals looking to stay out of sight of the general public. This makes it the ideal place for illegal marijuana growers. There are miles of unmarked roads and trails that weave their way through the forest. Looking for marijuana plants growing amongst the trees and brush is nearly impossible from the ground. However, as I previously discussed, we had some excellent pilots working for the agency and they knew what to look for when flying over the forest. Even when the growers tried to hide or cover the plants, the pilots were able to locate them.

One notable example of this also included something we had not seen before. I had an officer at the time who had been a sniper in the military and had served in Vietnam. That experience made him especially comfortable in the woods and gave him an eye for booby traps and dangers of all sorts. As he approached the grow operation from the ground, he spotted something no one else had seen. There was a piece of clear monofilament fishing line stretched across the walk-in trail, just above the ground. One end was tied to a tree, the other end was attached to the trigger of a loaded booby trap made with a 12-guage shotgun shell aimed at knee level on the trail. Any unsuspecting hiker, or in this case officer approaching the marijuana plants, who happened to trip the wire would have likely lost a leg from the close-quarters shotgun blast.

Imagine if some random hiker or bird watcher had unknowingly happened upon this trail. Imagine if it had been someone's child, out on a nature hike.

We dismantled the booby trap and made sure there were no others. We then uprooted and destroyed every marijuana plant in the area. The growers had assembled an irrigation system using PVC pipes and fifty-gallon drums of water that gravity-fed the pipes. Even though we never caught the people responsible, we eliminated their operation and cleared the entire forest of every marijuana plant we could find.

Ofc. Mike Thomas destroying marijuana plants. We located and destroyed countless marijuana grows over the years.

### *"Project Eagle"*

One of the goals I focused on during my time as a captain was finding ways for our officers and employees to interact with the general public, not just hunters, boaters, and fishermen. I wanted to help improve the agency's image and presence within the community.

Something all people could agree on was the problem of litter. No one likes to drive down the highway, hike down a trail, or go to their favorite swimming hole only to find a pile of garbage or litter strewn down the side of the road. It's also detrimental the fish and wildlife that rely on these areas.

After some lobbying with local businesses and the St. Johns Water Management District offices, we started a clean-up effort based entirely on volunteers from the community and the participating agencies. We hosted an event and spent the day cleaning up the waterways and parks in the area. We had hundreds of participants and support from sponsors. It became an annual event known as "Project Eagle". One of my lieutenants, Bruce Hanlin, headed the project and as a result, we received the "Keep Florida Beautiful Award" from TV host and conservationist, Jack Hannah.

We collected and disposed of thousands of bags of garbage and litter. We had hundreds of volunteers who spent hours in the hot sun picking up trash. The participation and response from the community was overwhelming.

Volunteers of all ages participated in the Project Eagle cleanup.

My second wife, Deana, and my step-daughter Melissa, also helped with the cleanup efforts.

## *"Fishing Opportunities"*

One of the things I noticed immediately about my area when I arrived was the lack of designated fishing areas on the freshwater bodies of the state. Unlike the freshwater areas, the saltwater fishing opportunities were plentiful. Every bridge or park located on the saltwater side had a pier or fishing platform and a parking lot. However, there were very few docks or designated fishing piers on the lakes and rivers in my area. There were parks and boat ramps, but not many piers or docks.

At the time, I knew a very influential individual who was appointed by the Governor as head of the roadways commission. I brought the disparity to his attention and asked him why the state thought saltwater fishing was more important than freshwater fishing.

"Well, it really isn't," he responded.

So, he told me he would take care of it.

I also brought the issue up with our agency commissioners. They serve on the commission as volunteers because, much like our employees, they share a passion for the issues that face our natural resources. They also carry a great deal of influence in the political and business community in our Capitol. A couple months thereafter, I received a call from my friend informing me that the roadways commission would be setting aside some money for freshwater bridges and piers. What began as only a couple locations became a great increase in the number of fishing piers, docks, and parks across the state.

This issue was near and dear to my heart because as I grew up fishing with my grandmother in the lakes around Sumter County, we were too poor to afford a boat and we often found ourselves fishing from the bank in the few locations that were accessible to us. Sometimes this meant fishing in a ditch or creek, surrounded by high weeds, snakes, and ticks.

One of my lieutenants, who also wrote an excellent book detailing his adventures as a game warden, was Bob Lee. He headed up a program in Putnam County, partnered with the Bassmasters group, which sponsored a fishing program that encouraged young people to get outdoors and go fishing. We focused on the families of single parents in an effort to develop a love of the outdoors and create recreational opportunities for children who were less fortunate. Having come from a divorced family myself, I understood the need for a program like this one.

This was just one of the many fishing events we sponsored across the state.

## *"Working with Our Biologists"*

I always enjoyed working with the biologists employed by the agency. It was always educational, often enjoyable, and sometimes exciting. I also always encouraged my officers to do so in order to maintain the interagency relationships between our departments and to help my officers learn more about the animals and resources they were tasked with protecting. I know I certainly learned a great deal from our biologists over the years and it made me a better officer and supervisor.

The Ocala National Forest has one of the largest populations black bears in the state of Florida. State Road 40 runs from the Gulf of Mexico, across the state from Ocala east to the Atlantic coast at Ormond and Daytona Beach. The biggest cause of death for the bears at the time was being struck by a vehicle.

Our biologists were documenting and monitoring the bear population in an attempt to find a way to minimize their deaths at the hands of motorists.  I had joined them to help them capture and tag a young black bear just off the highway.

When asked, I always told the public that bears were more afraid of us than we were of them. At the time, there had been no confirmed documented incidents of bears attacking people in the state, although there have since been a few. I think a big part of protecting any animal, especially a predator, is convincing the general public that they are not a threat to people.

We didn't realize that this young bear was still with his mother. While working on the young bear and attempting to place a

**187**

tag and tracking collar on it, the mother approached us from behind and before we noticed, she was within 10 feet of us and throwing a fit.

We've all heard the saying "You don't mess with Mama bear". It's not a joke.

Thankfully, she didn't charge us, but I was as scared in that moment as I had ever been. I certainly didn't want to have to shoot that Mama bear. We stepped away and waited for the young bear to recover from the sedative it was given. Both bears walked away and no one was harmed.

## "The Exotic Species of Florida"

If you spend any time at all in the woods or on the waters of Florida, you will eventually encounter one of the many exotic animals that have been introduced by humans over the years. It is obvious to most people that a tiger or an elephant does not belong in Florida, but there are many other species that have invaded into the natural habitats of Florida's native fauna that people are not aware of.

South Florida has a huge problem with invasive and exotic fish and reptile species. Snakehead fish, which are very aggressive and eat almost all other fish, have become prolific and wiped out many native fish species in bodies of water on the southern tip of the peninsula. Burmese pythons have established a large population in south Florida and have spread northward through the Everglades. The agency is actively hunting and eradicating this large breed snake. Several species of lizard, including monitors and iguanas, have also established large populations around the state. They compete with native species for habitat and food.

Thankfully, many of these invasive animals are contained to South Florida and its warm sub-tropical climate.

One species, however, has taken over a portion of the Ocala National Forest around the Ocklawaha River and the Silver River, home to one of Florida's greatest natural treasures, Silver Springs.

In the 1940's and 1950's, Silver Springs was a popular tourist attraction and a desirable filming location for several TV shows and movie films. The landscape resembles a dense jungle and is easily accessed by film crews and production companies who didn't want to spend the money on a trip to Africa. Unfortunately, it didn't have the animals needed to make the scenery as accurate as the African jungle. The solution? Bring in the monkeys.

Rhesus macaques are native to parts of Asia and Africa. They are a large breed of monkey that are easily captured and bred in captivity. In order to make the scenery more realistic for viewers and tourists, the monkeys were brought into Silver Springs and placed on an island. At the time, it was believed that the monkeys could not swim and would remain trapped on the island. It turned out, Rhesus macaques are one of the few species of monkey that are excellent swimmers and they are quite at home in the water. It didn't take long for the monkeys to spread through the park and into the surrounding areas.

Over the years, attempts to control their numbers by trapping them have been of little or no success. The macaques are very intelligent, and they quickly learned to avoid capture.

The monkeys will eat almost anything, including the eggs of protected and endangered species of birds that nest along the river. The monkeys are aggressive, and they have been known to attack people in boats and raid camp sites. The macaques are known carriers of the Herpes virus, as well as Hepatitis and HIV.

Once it became apparent that the monkeys were having a drastic effect on bird numbers and their activity was causing a very serious public hazard, the state was left with no other option. Despite some public outcry and multiple protests to "leave the monkeys alone" because "monkey lives matter", the agency adopted a policy of eradicating the monkeys. Several times a year, groups of biologists would travel out and shoot the monkeys, hoping to control their numbers. Even though this worked to an extent, there are still several large troops of Rhesus macaques living along the Ocklawaha and Silver rivers, and they are frequently observed along the river's edge harassing tourists, hikers, campers, and boaters.

**Rhesus Macaques**

## "Scared of the Dark"

Not everyone we hired was cut out for the job. Sometimes, as a supervisor, you just have to help your employees move on to other things because it isn't working out.

One of my lieutenants was promoted and before his vacant position could be filled, I had to serve as the direct supervisor for his group of officers. I decided that I would get out and work with these officers to see how they were doing and get to know them a little better.

I took one officer, who will remain nameless, on a ride along one night to work fire hunters. As we commonly did, in order to cover a large area with fewer people, we split up. I dropped him off at one end of a stretch of highway and I drove some ways up the road and set up. I told him that if he saw a likely suspect to signal me with his flashlight and I would pull out to block the road with our vehicle.

We hadn't even been set up an hour when he came walking up.

"What you need? You need a drink or something?"

"No," he replied, "I just ain't sitting down there by myself.

"What?!" I couldn't believe what my ears had just heard.

"Yeah, I'm not gonna be sitting down there all by myself."

"Ok," I calmly agreed, "Get in the car."

We loaded up and I took him back to his vehicle. That was the last time he worked for me. I heard that a short time later, he took a job with a Sheriff's Office as a deputy, and by all accounts did a really good job.

The life of a wildlife officer can be lonely and dark at times. It isn't something that everyone can do.

## *"Taking a Leak"*

It seems like such a simple thing, but I noticed over the years that one of the most important things I could do before beginning a detail or setting up to catch a law breaker, was to take a leak.

If I ever got involved in a car chase or a boat chase, or I was ever hiding and observing for hours on end, it wasn't always possible to stop and relieve myself. High stress situations can make a person very nervous and it was not unheard of for someone to pee their pants when involved in a chase or a fight. So, I always made sure to pee before I got started.

One night, I was patrolling timber country near Cross City. The timber companies always constructed their own lumber bridges to cross creeks or canals between timber cuts. Back then, it was common practice to drive around with no headlights as to avoid detection. I felt comfortable in my knowledge of the area and could still see pretty good in the moonlight. For most people, it takes a few seconds for their eyes to adjust to the darkness. Once a person's pupils open up, they can see relatively well in the dark with only the ambient light from the moon and stars.

I had been in and out of the area several times in the previous few days, and I knew I was coming up on ditch that was about 40 feet across with one such timber bridge. I decided to stop and take a leak before crossing the bridge, and I didn't want to pull out into the open area on the other side of the bridge. So, I parked my car and walked through the darkness to where I was certain the bridge began.

I was well into a full stream when I was startled by a holler.

**"Hey!!! What in the hell?!?!"**

I scrambled around, pants still unzipped, and pulled out my flashlight. I was very surprised to find that the timber company had removed the bridge completely that very same day.

To make matters even more disturbing, two men, who had been drinking and were very drunk, had driven their Cadillac convertible off the bridge and landed flat on all four tires, squarely at the bottom in about a foot or two of water. Apparently too drunk to do anything about it that night, they decided to sleep it off right there where they had landed. I had just peed all over them and into their Cadillac.

"Holy crap! Are ya'll alright?"

"Yeah," one man replied, "except for the fact that you're peeing on me!"

The fact that I stopped to take a leak saved a couple lives that night. Yeah, I peed on him, but if I had not stopped, I would have run off the same drop and killed both those men with my squad car.

Strangely enough, years later it happened again!

One of my favorite things to do while working in the Ocala National Forest was drive up on one of the higher ridges and park in the dark. I would just sit and listen, and I could see for miles in either direction. If a gunshot rang out or a spotlight swept through the woods, I would know it immediately.

So, one night, as I had done countless times before, I made my way up the hill on one of the many dirt roads scattered around the forest. Usually, with my headlights off, I would drive to the tip top of the hill and wait, but this night (for whatever reason) I decided to stop about 40 yards shy of the hilltop to take a leak.

As I was standing there draining my bladder, I began to see several large dark objects against the light sand background of the road ahead of me. I squinted and watched for a few seconds, thinking maybe they were bears, but they didn't move and made no noise.

I couldn't figure out what they were and I didn't want to just walk up on them, so I reached down through the driver's side window and flipped on my headlights.

There, laying in the middle of the road, were at least 30 people in sleeping bags, dead asleep. If I had done what I usually did and drove to the top of the hill, I would have run over and probably killed 3 or 4 of them before stopping.

I hit the button for my siren.

"WHOOOOOOOOOOOOPP!"

Startled, they all popped up off the road like a bunch of bundled up whack-a-moles.

"What they hell is going on? What are ya'll doin' laying in the middle of the damn road? I could have killed you all!"

"We are from the University of Florida," replied the professor in charge of the group. "We are with the astronomy department. We come out her a couple times a year to get away from the city lights and observe the stars."

I was a bit disturbed knowing that I had just come within a few feet of killing some college kids.

"Are you serious? Don't you think maybe it would be a good idea to move over to the side of the road a bit?"

They agreed and moved off to the shoulder of the road. Again, you just never know what you'll run into, or over, out there.

Since then, it has become agency policy that officers are no longer permitted to drive without their headlights on. This practice led to several incidents of property damage over the years, and in one tragic accident, the death of two of our officers in south Florida.

## "Green Turtle Eggs on The Black Market"

As I have said many times, if you're going to be an outlaw, you need to be careful who you make angry, especially friends and family. On countless occasions, vindictive family members and friends will let their anger get the better of them, often resulting in very detailed and incriminating information being handed to us.

We received a complaint from an informant letting us know that their estranged friend was harvesting green turtle eggs in the Canaveral National Seashore, a U.S. National Park. They also claimed that he was poaching alligators as well, and selling both the eggs and gator meat to anyone looking to buy.

It didn't take long to set up a sting operation using an undercover officer posing as a buyer. We set up the meeting in the National Park and true to the informant's word, the man showed up with a cooler full of green turtle eggs and gator meat. The man was also selling the gator hides.

We made the arrest and the case was fairly straight forward. Interestingly enough, the man wasn't just cornering the local market. He was selling to buyers in Texas, who were in turn smuggling the eggs into Canada, where they were then filtered back into the U.S., supplying several high-end restaurants in New York City.

Given the nature of the charges and the scope of what we uncovered, we turned the case over to the U.S. Fish and Wildlife Service. The man ended up serving several years in prison.

Green Sea Turtle eggs in the
nest on a Florida beach.

### "My Least Favorite Part of the Job"

Something no first responder enjoys is recovering the body of a deceased person. This is especially true in drowning cases. Often times, drowning victims are not immediately found because of wind, current, and water clarity conditions.

One practice I implemented as a supervisor was that we would never stop searching for a victim until they were found. Other agencies would postpone a search because of darkness or weather. I made sure we continued our searches until the person was located. Imagine if it was your loved one who was missing. I know that if it were my family member, I wouldn't want anyone to stop looking.

Another protocol that I put an end to was the use of drag hooks. Often, if a body was not immediately located or the water conditions made it impossible to put divers in the water, a drag hook was used. Sometimes, bodies would be in the water for several days. Animal activity and natural decomposition could sometimes make the use of a hook a very destructive proposition for the victim's body. This often meant more work for us, but we wanted to be as respectful and caring of the victims as we could in our recovery efforts. We wanted to preserve the victim as much as we could for identification and funeral purposes. We also made sure to never bring a body back to a boat ramp or shoreline where civilians, media members, or family members were located. When necessary, we would take the medical examiner out on our boat to recover and take possession of the body.

We also were one of the first agencies in the country to

implement a program that used dogs to detect bodies in the water. Because of Hollywood movies and stories that show fleeing prisoners and escapees running through swamps and water, many people falsely believe that water eliminates human scent making it difficult for dogs to track. The opposite is actually true. Water can sometimes preserve or concentrate the scent of a body. Once the dogs are trained, they are very effective at locating submerged bodies. On more than one occasion, a K-9 officer was able to locate the exact location of a drowning victim in total darkness. Once the dog alerted on a spot at the surface, a diver was able to quickly recover the body from the water.

Looking for deceased individuals can be a very stressful event for a law enforcement officer. When the person was a child, the effects of searching for and recovering a victim can be profound. Many officers have needed counseling to deal with the grief and stress that followed the recovery of a child victim.

I only mention this to illuminate an aspect of the job that many people simply aren't aware of. Looking for a missing child, or having to notify a family of the death of a loved one is something no person ever wants to do. In events like these, it always meant a great deal to me to have the gratitude and appreciation of the families of the deceased. They would often thank us for our hard work, professionalism, and dedication to recovering their loved ones.

Another aspect unique to the job of a wildlife officer is investigating hunting accidents. It goes without saying that any sport or activity involving firearms can result in accidents and death. Even though hunters are well-known for their skills and safety with the use of firearms, rare tragedies do occur.

There were several cases over the years that resulted in the death of a hunter, and sometimes the death of a child or grandchild.

One of the more tragic examples involved a grandfather who was hunting with his young grandson, who was sitting on his lap. The grandfather heard a loud "POP" and his grandson fell over. A hunter near them had mistaken the grandson's movement as a turkey in the brush and shot the child in the head, killing him instantly.

Another incident involved a father who had accidentally shot his own son while driving in the woods. There was a loaded rifle in a gun rack on the rear window of their truck. When they ran over a rough spot in the road, the rifle fell from the rack. When he attempted to catch the falling gun, the father accidentally shot his son in the passenger seat.

Another problem we occasionally encountered was suicide by cop. For whatever reason, over the years, it became more common for suicidal individuals to seek out police officers to shoot and kill them when they didn't feel they could do it themselves. To avoid being found by their loved ones or friends, they would often travel out to secluded wilderness areas, which increased the likelihood that we would encounter them. This happened several times throughout the state, including once to one of my officers. When my officer approached the man merely to speak to him, he began firing shots from a handgun at the officer. He then killed himself.

Thankfully, stories like these are very few and far between, but they still show how the day to day events our officers experience can have a profound influence on their mental well-being and the community as a whole.

One of our K-9 officers, Mike Fisher, working with his dog Sonny, trained to find the bodies of drowning victims, below the surface of the water.

## "Lucky Cases"

Sometimes, it's just better to be lucky than good. Many of the cases we made were just a result of being in the right place at the right time. I always believed in the saying, "Luck is what happens when preparation meets opportunity." This proved to be true more than once.

I was on patrol one night when I passed what I thought was a broken-down vehicle. I was on a new bypass road they had just finished around Daytona. I wasn't really expecting much to be happening in that area, but since it had never been patrolled, I decided to check it out.

As I drove by, it looked like two men were bent over in the ditch. I figured they had lost a wheel and were retrieving it from the brush along the roadway. Hoping I could assist, and probably a little bored, I stopped to make sure they were doing alright. What I found was two men dragging a doe deer out of the ditch. They had spotted the deer as they were driving by and had quickly taken the shot. I just happened to drive up at the worst possible moment for them. Another 30 seconds earlier or later, I would have missed the entire event.

Another time, not far from there on SR 40, I drove by a group of men on horseback in a timber block alongside the highway. Again, I just happened to be driving by at the perfect moment. I spotted the men through the trees, just off the road, heading in the opposite direction. It wasn't hunting season and even though riding horses wasn't illegal, I suspected maybe they were hunting anyway.

The road was busy and there were plenty of cars travelling in either direction. I didn't figure they would be paying much attention to the traffic. Hoping they hadn't spotted me, I continued down the road a bit, turned around and came back to a cut road just ahead of where I thought the men would pop out of the woods. I hid my car and waited in the bushes. It wasn't long before their dogs, followed closely by the riders carrying rifles, emerged within only a few yards of my position. They had no idea I was there until I had already grabbed one of the horses by the bridle.

"What are ya'll doing," I asked, nearly scaring one rider clean off his horse.

"Oh! Not much, just looking around."

"Really?" Immediately I noticed one of the men had some blood on his pant leg and some on his boot.

It didn't take much questioning to get the men to confess to killing the deer and hiding it some ways back from where I stopped them. I made the arrests, recovered the deer, and for some time after that, I was known as "Mr. Lucky". My officers there wanted me to stay out of their area. They thought I was trying to take all their cases, which wasn't the case at all. It was just dumb luck.

One of the luckiest moments of my career happened when I was sitting in my car on a quiet rainy night, just south of Ft. McCoy in Marion County. It was late and I was just hoping to find anyone out or to maybe hear a shot in the distance.

I didn't have to wait long. I clearly heard two or three gunshots from a small caliber rifle. They seemed to be no more than a mile to the west of my position, so I slowly traveled in my patrol vehicle with my lights off, hoping to run across the person responsible for the shots. After traveling over 3 miles, I was certain they had escaped.

Then, a vehicle popped out of a dirt trail onto the road in front of me. It was a hunter exiting the woods. I knew given the late hour that he was up to no good, but the only sign of any violation was some blood in the bed of his truck. No deer, no gun.

After a short interview with the very nervous man, he admitted to killing a doe deer and that the deer and the gun were now on their way to Palatka in his friend's truck.

I quickly radioed the nearest officer and they easily located the other hunter on his way back home, seizing the deer and the gun.

While I was writing the hunter his ticket, another pickup truck pulled out into the road from a private ranch gate less than a hundred yards away. Not one to pass up the opportunity, I stopped the vehicle. In the bed of the truck were several dead alligators. The driver had recently shot them in the swamp with a friend aboard their airboat, and he was transporting them back to his home.

It was in fact this poacher's gunshots I had heard from over 3 miles away, as he shot the gators with his .22 caliber rifle. If not for the timing of those shots, I would never had seen the deer poacher. If not for stopping the deer poacher, I would never had seen the gator outlaw. I was just lucky to be in the right place at the right time. Unfortunately for the outlaws, the opposite was true.

It's hard to deny being a gator poacher when you are caught red handed, with a load of dead gators in your truck.

## "If You Have Enough Money"

During hunting season, the Ocala National Forest fills with hundreds of hunters from all over the state and country. At the time, we simply didn't have enough officers to work all the areas we needed to cover, so I made a point of making sure I was available and in the field to assist and patrol with my crews.

After you gain several seasons worth of experience, you just sort of get a feel for which people are up to no good. You start to notice little things, like behaviors patterns in how they operate, that clue you in to what is going on.

I had learned that a great way to check large numbers of hunters in the forest was not to seek them out. You could spend a great deal of time, energy, and gasoline running around the forest looking for every hunter you could locate.

Instead, I found that parking at intersections around the forest and using makeshift checkpoints allowed me to stop more people. The roads naturally funneled them to me and I could change positions randomly to avoid becoming predictable in my patrols.

On one opening weekend, I set up at an intersection I knew would be busy. I never stopped every car. It just wasn't feasible. There were simply too many to check them all single handed. So, I picked the ones I thought looked most likely to have violations.

That day, I saw a convoy of trucks and trailers coming out of the forest headed towards me. I let the first few go by with a wave, when I noticed the driver of the fourth vehicle trying real hard to not look at me. This was almost always a sure sign of a guilty conscience. It was a nice, newer truck with a very nice camper behind it. I stopped the vehicle and immediately new there was a problem. The man was noticeably nervous and agitated. A quick search of his trailer revealed why. He had killed a doe deer...something that was illegal at that point in the season.

The case was fairly straight forward. I asked the man where he lived and he said that he lived in Volusia county.

In those days, in lieu of making an arrest, we could accept cash bonds from a suspect. This meant we could issue a notice to appear in court and they would never have to bond out of jail. If they didn't show up for the court date, the cash was enough to cover any fine they would incur if they were found guilty. I was never comfortable accepting cash from suspects. I always made a point of placing it in my shirt pocket as opposed to placing it in my billfold. Most of the time, people wouldn't carry enough cash to pay the bond amount, so it usually wasn't an issue.

Seeing as how this man lived in Volusia and owned a business there, I was fairly confident he would show up for court. I told him that I knew where to find him if he didn't. I mentioned to him that he could pay the bond amount up front, not expecting that he would fork over the $500 cash that accompanied that specific crime.

"That won't be a problem," he plainly stated.

**209**

He then proceeded to pull out what must have been three or four thousand dollars' worth of hundreds from his front pants pocket and casually peeled off five bills. Even these days, $500 is not chump change, but in those days, it was rare to see that much cash floating around, especially out in the woods. I wrote the ticket and gave the man his court date.

"If I don't show up to court, will that cover the fine?"

"Yeah," I replied, "That will pretty well cover it."

"OK then."

The man folded up his ticket, loaded back up in his truck, and went on his way. It just goes to show how having money can make dealing with your problems that much simpler, especially when you're a criminal.

## "Artifact Hunters"

I have always had a great personal interest in the Seminole people, and all Native American tribes of North America. I feel like they are historically some of the most mistreated people. We took their property and lands, enslaved many of them, slaughtered thousands of them in the process, and introduced diseases that wiped out countless others. Their culture has always been fascinating to me and played a huge role in the history of the state of Florida and the entire country.

The state is covered with archeological sites, many of which are located on or near the lakes, rivers, and estuaries that the native people relied upon for food and travel. These sites are protected by law and disturbing them is not only a crime, but incredibly disrespectful to the native peoples. Imagine...how would you feel if someone dug up your great grandfather's grave to take his rings or his wrist watch?

Since our officers spend a great deal of time on these waterways, it is inevitable that we run across people hunting for artifacts and digging up these sites.

One particular example of this was a case made by Officer Danton Jones. In one of the biggest cases ever made along the Ocklawaha River, Danton discovered several men digging in the river bank and collecting artifacts from a gravesite. The holes were so large and deep that as he approached them, all officer jones could see was dirt being thrown up from the holes. The diggers were completely concealed inside the holes.

They had already collected dozens of artifacts. Once the case was made, those artifacts were turned over to the University of Florida and are now part of the exhibit at the Natural History Museum there.

Typical arrowheads found by artifact hunters along the river banks are valued by both collectors and researchers.

## "The Decline of Commercial Fishing"

After I had been on the St. Johns River for a time, it became apparent that we needed to develop a better relationship with the commercial fishermen all along the river. Often times, interactions between our officers and commercial fishermen resulted in the fisherman fleeing and the officer giving chase. These high-speed chases were often very dangerous, as the fishermen knew the waters very well and would often try to lure the officers into obstacles along the river, resulting in property damage and potentially injury or death. There were lift nets along the river. These large nets were attached to poles at the surface of the water and if you didn't know it was there, a lift net could stop and destroy a speeding boat in a hurry, potentially sending an officer flying through the air and into the river.

I brought to the attention of the brass in Tallahassee that the specific law that addressed fleeing and eluding did not cover vessels at the time. I wanted to make sure that the law matched the severity of the crime and that the appropriate punishment was handed down, especially if one of my officers was ever hurt. So, they lobbied the Legislature and were successful in getting the law passed.

I also understood that these fishermen were just trying to make a living and that ultimately, it was in all our best interests to see eye to eye as best we could.

So, I got the idea of putting together a fish fry. I contacted the president of the Organized Fishermen of Florida (OFF) in Welaka. We set up the cookout and got everyone together.

They furnished the fish and even though some of them were unhappy about it, my officers in the area attended the meeting. I wanted to make sure they understood the new law and the severity of the situation, and why we were doing what we were doing.

*"We aren't playing games anymore. We aren't going to be risking lives and property on this river over some fish. The law is the law, and if you continue to do this, it's going to have some serious consequences. Someone is going to get killed and that just isn't something we can have happen. If it does, we are going to take everything you have and pursue it to the farthest extent of the law. We are talking about serious prison time. For what? Some fish?"*

It got their attention.

Another important step in developing these relationships was integrating my officers into the community. One of the best I had was Bob Lee. Bob did a wonderful job bringing around the commercial fishing community around Palatka and Welaka, and his efforts went a long way towards helping us be successful in our efforts. He got to know most of the fishermen while working for me and was a well-known part of that community for years. He actually ended up joining the Volunteer Fire Department. I can't say enough about what he accomplished there.

All of this worked to some extent. We still had those who wanted to flee, and our officers were great at catching them...sometimes. But for the most part, the relationship improved dramatically.

Eventually however, the times changed. The advent of commercial freshwater fish farms led to a severe decline in fish prices, making commercial freshwater fishing a more difficult way to make a living. High demand for fish and restaurants wanting a more consistent product in both taste and availability placed a great deal of strain on the industry. Today, most of the fish served in these places is farm raised and sadly, the heyday of commercial freshwater fishing has since passed. There are still a few around the St. Johns, but their numbers are limited.

## "The Last Airboat Chase"

As a captain, I always tried to pass on any intel or information to my lieutenants and their officers so that they could work the case and make an arrest. It wasn't that I didn't want to work the cases, but I wanted to make sure they gained the experience and had the opportunity to be successful, in their own right.

I had heard a rumor about some potential monkey fishing taking place on the Ocklawaha River. The Ocklawaha winds and curves its way through the Ocala National Forest like a long dark snake. It's a very narrow and shallow river and is filled with logs and snags that make navigating it in broad daylight tricky, and almost impossible at night.

Since all my officers were busy doing other things, I decided to take one of our reservists with me and go for an airboat ride on the river. More than anything, I wanted to do some recon of the area and just see what was going on. I didn't expect to stop and check any boats on a late weeknight.

We decided to go and sit for a bit in the area where the supposed monkey fishing was taking place. As I mentioned before, I always found you could catch more poachers with your ears than your eyes. So, we made our way up into one of the many feeder creeks that runs into the Ocklawaha. I took an old surplus parachute and covered the aluminum deck of the airboat to hide it from anyone who may pass by while working a spotlight.

It was about 2 a.m. when we heard a boat idling up the river, coming directly towards us.

"Putt, putt, putt, putt, putt..."

The boat made the turn from the main river channel directly into the creek we were hiding in. He was completely blacked out, running without navigation lights or spot lights. This was another dead giveaway that he was up to no good.

I knew that this was often how the fisherman would work the monkey machine. As they idled into the current, they would crank the machine to stun the fish. After doing this for a few minutes, they would stop to drift with the current, pull out a dip net, and gather the stunned fish. It was an incredibly effective way to catch a large number of fish. It was also highly illegal.

Most of our confrontations with monkey fishermen ended with a high-speed chase. Their boats, most of which were hand-made skipjacks with large, powerful motors, were perfect for running the skinny waters of the river and were built for maneuverability and speed.

We sat there, in silence in the dark as he approached.

Fully expecting him to flee as soon as he became aware of our presence, I had one hand on the boat ignition, waiting to crank the engine as soon as I needed to. My airboat didn't always crank on the first try, and in my mind, I was hoping it did in this instance.

He continued up the creek until he was no more than 4 or 5 feet from the bow of our boat.

"OH HELLLLLLLL!!!!"

It was always entertaining, the reactions we would get, when the poachers happened upon us.

How he managed to do a complete 180 degrees turn in that tiny creek with his 18-foot boat is beyond me. Immediately, the chase was on. I turned the key and my boat's engine roared to life.

The fisherman jammed the throttle of his 150-horsepower motor and he was off. He quickly put a hundred yards or so between his boat and ours. Fortunately for us, he was forced to run the winding main channel of the river, as the inside of every hairpin turn on the river was filled with logs that could have torn the transom off the back of his boat had he been unlucky enough to snag his motor on one.

However, our airboat was not as burdened by the river as his vessel was. I was able to cut the inside of every turn, as my airboat easily glided over and bounced off the floating logs and shallow sand bars. This probably wasn't the safest way to run the river, but I wanted so badly to catch this poacher. Like a pit bull, I wasn't about to let him get away. Riding in our airboat, we were high above the water's surface and this meant that every low-hanging branch was smacking us in the face as we sped down the river channel.

After about a mile, I caught up to the fleeing fisherman and forced him to the river's edge. At some point in time during the chase, he had dumped his monkey fishing machine, and even though we searched for several hours, we never found it.

**218**

I issued the man several citations for his multiple violations, including one for fleeing and eluding, and sent him home with a court date.

When we made it back to the ramp to load the airboat back on the trailer, we realized we were a bit scratched up. Our uniforms had been torn and ruined by the low hanging branches along the river as we passed through them during the chase.

We finished loading the boat and as we stood there at the ramp under the glow of the parking lot light, I noticed something on the head of my reservist.

"Hey, what is that...on your head there?"

He reached up and felt it.

"OW!!! What in the hell?!?!"

At some point during the chase, we must have hit a tree branch that was holding a large, top-water fishing lure that had broken off from some unlucky fisherman's line.

The lure, which had three large, barbed treble hooks on it, was now securely embedded in the scalp of my reservist, on the top of his forehead right at his hairline.

With all the excitement and adrenaline, he hadn't noticed the pain of the lure now dangling from his head. Luckily, the hooks hadn't gone all the way past the barbs and we easily removed it from his skin. We put a little antiseptic on it and everything was fine...but for some reason, despite my invitations, that was the last airboat ride he would ever go on with me.

Despite my somewhat checkered airboating history, my step-son Garrett has accompanied me on many fish gigging trips. I am happy to say, he returned unharmed almost every time. Here he is with a large gar fish he gigged.

## "Hunters and Anti-Hunters"

One of the stranger aspects of my job was needing to protect hunters and hunter rights from anti-hunters and animal rights activist groups. Anytime we had an organized hunting event, the vocal anti-hunting groups would protest and even take actions to prevent or stop the hunts.

One year, we helped organize an English-style fox hunting event in which the riders would work their dogs to chase a fox through the woods. There was actually a penalty of expulsion from the hunt for anyone who harmed a fox. The event was more of a show than a hunt.

Before the event, a group of animal rights and anti-hunting activist formed to protest the hunt. They even went as far to threaten placing roofing nails on the trails the horses would be using. That never made much sense to me. If you love the animals that much, why hurt the horses?

No foxes were ever killed. I'm happy to say that no one was arrested and no animals were harmed by either group.

Don't get me wrong. I understand the love of animals. You also should understand that hunters and sportsmen love animals as well. There's a place and a purpose for hunting in our society. As animal populations grow because of disease control and conservation efforts, hunting serves to control those populations in a humane and conservative way. Large numbers of deer need to be controlled to avoid disease within the herd and to lessen accidents involving deer and automobiles.

Deer populations exploded in Florida when U.F. biologists found a way to eradicate screw worms, much as they did the fruit fly. Screw worms were the larvae of a type of fly that laid its eggs in the open wounds of animals. When a male deer was in velvet and scraping his horns, or a baby deer was a newborn and the navel had not yet healed, those flies would lay their eggs and the animal would literally be eaten alive by the worms if left untreated. This decimated not only livestock numbers, but wildlife populations as well.

Today, even though hunting has declined somewhat, hunters still play an important role in the conservation of our natural resources and wildlife.

I have recently seen incidents involving protesters harassing and interrupting fishermen and their children. We have laws that address this issue and the agency is happy to enforce them.

### *"Don't Run Over Your Evidence"*

Two of the best officers I ever had were involved in one of the funniest incidents I ever heard about. Billy Walker, who now works for the U.S. Marshall's Office, and Andy Krauss, who is now a major in Lake City, both came out of the academy together and worked for me in Marion County.

They had recently gotten off probation and were excited about being able to work together without having to be constantly supervised. Like most new officers, they were chomping at the bit, ready to go.

One night, they decided to work fire hunters on Highway 19 near Salt Springs. They pulled off the highway and hid their car, waiting for some action. Not long into it, a car came by and as they watched, the car's brake lights lit up.

"POW!"

The occupants of the car had shot a deer about half a mile up the road from Andy and Billy. Ecstatic, they hopped in the car and the chase was on. As they pulled out to pursue the suspects, they made a single rookie mistake: they flipped on the blue light on their patrol vehicle.

This immediately caused the offenders to flee and they already had a half mile head start.

With the pedal to the floor, Billy and Andy were in hot pursuit. As soon as they reached the spot where the car had stopped, they heard and felt a strange "THUMP THUMP."

**223**

"What was that," Andy asked.

Billy responded, "I'm pretty sure that was their deer."

The two new officers had just run over their biggest piece of evidence. Not wanting to let the poachers escape and figuring they could return for the deer later, they followed the offenders into Salt Springs.

The fleeing car turned off the main paved road and down a side dirt road, into a small area with several homes. As they rolled up, Billy and Andy assumed the occupants had fled on foot and quickly searched the area. Finding no sign of the poachers, they returned to the vehicle. A quick search with the flashlight revealed both men, hiding underneath the car. In their excitement to get after them, Andy and Billy had initially walked right by the hiding suspects. They made the arrests and issued both men citations for fire hunting and fleeing. Then, they made their way back to retrieve the deer.

Unfortunately, in the few minutes between hitting the deer and apprehending the men, someone had stopped and retrieved the deer. The people of Salt Springs are smart enough to know you don't pass up a free lunch.

All that was left was a few scrapes of fur and some blood in the road.

Either way, the case was made.

That could have happened to anybody, even me. But I always found that to be one the most humorous situations any of my officers were ever involved in.

**224**

A poached deer, taken as evidence.

### *"My Retirement"*

I've told quite a few of the more memorable stories from a career that spanned more than 3 decades. These stories are some of my fondest memories, and I hope you have enjoyed reading these stories as much as I have enjoyed telling them.

My original goal when writing this book was to share some of my adventures and shed a little light on some of the lesser known aspects of the job. I also wanted to leave these stories for my great grandchildren so that they would know what their great grandad did as a game warden back in the old days.

When I got to be about 61 years old, I started looking back on my 35-plus years with the agency. That last airboat chase got me to thinking:

"You know, that wasn't the smartest thing I had ever done."

My reaction times weren't what they used to be.

Realizing that we had a new generation of young officers who were more than capable of carrying the torch, and feeling secure in what I had accomplished in my career, I decided it was time to retire. I knew I would miss the job and more than anything, I loved and respected the people I had been privileged to work with.

At that point, I'd had several operations, battled cancer, and injured myself countless times. I had injured both shoulders during defensive tactics training with other officers. After that, I learned to pick the smallest as a partner, or the female officer because I knew she would take it easy on me. I just wasn't as

**226**

flexible or as strong as I used to be. Time catches up with all of us. There was no question that this was a young person's job and I was no longer a young person.

The job, too, had changed. The vast wilderness areas had dwindled from development and many wildlife areas had become suburban communities. For a multitude of reasons, the number of fire hunting cases dropped. I suspect it was a combination of fewer opportunities to fire hunt without being caught by one of our officers and fewer areas that one could hunt multitudes of deer. There are homes and communities everywhere these days. With cellphones in every pocket, a gunshot rarely goes unreported. I also think that as the sport of hunting has evolved over the years, sportsmen (and sportswomen) have realized there is no sport in shooting an illegal deer.

I still have a great many stories to share and maybe one day I'll write another book. I know I have been blessed by God, and through my faith, I was fortunate to have lived through these adventures relatively unharmed. I'm glad I never had to take the life of another person while performing my duties.

Finally, I would challenge every reader to find a conservation cause to join, regardless of where you are or what your political affiliation is. I have learned over the years that no matter what your cause, when people work together they are stronger and more influential. There are countless examples of how conservation groups have successfully brought species and resources back from the brink of extinction and ruin. Without these groups, we wouldn't have manatees, panthers, bald eagles, alligators, or many of the other species that now thrive in the Florida wilderness. As our world becomes more crowded, we should all seek to conserve our precious natural resources so that future generations can enjoy them as we have. Good luck and for the sake of our future generations, take a kid fishing.

-Captain Wayne King

Captain Wayne King is retired and lives on his farm in Ft. McCoy, Florida. He spends his time with his with family and friends. Along with taking part in the occasional cattle roundup, he enjoys giving airboat rides and showing his passengers the "real Florida".
Photo, c.2018

# Florida Fish and Wildlife Conservation Commission

## Fallen in the Line of Duty – Officer Down Memorial Page (www.odmp.org)

Lieutenant Joseph A. Martyna
Florida Fish and Wildlife Conservation Commission
EOW: Sunday, November 16, 2008
Cause: Heart attack

Wildlife Officer Michelle A. Lawless
Florida Fish and Wildlife Conservation Commission
EOW: Saturday, October 27, 2007
Cause: Accidental

Lieutenant Delmar Teagan
Florida Fish and Wildlife Conservation Commission
EOW: Friday, April 13, 2007
Cause: Automobile crash

Wildlife Officer Charles T. Randall
Florida Fish and Wildlife Conservation Commission
EOW: Sunday, October 28, 2001
Cause: Automobile crash

Wildlife Officer Roy R. Burnsed
Florida Fish and Wildlife Conservation Commission
EOW: Friday, October 26, 2001
Cause: Automobile crash

Wildlife Officer Ray Lynn Barnes
Florida Game and Fresh Water Fish Commission
EOW: Saturday, November 21, 1987
Cause: Gunfire

Wildlife Officer Margaret E. "Peggy" Park
Florida Game and Fresh Water Fish Commission
EOW: Thursday, December 13, 1984
Cause: Gunfire

Wildlife Officer Danese Byron Crowder
Florida Game and Fresh Water Fish Commission
EOW: Friday, May 3, 1974
Cause: Gunfire

Wildlife Officer James L. Cook
Florida Game and Fresh Water Fish Commission
EOW: Friday, December 8, 1972
Cause: Drowned

Sergeant Harry Charles Chapin
Florida Game and Fresh Water Fish Commission
EOW: Sunday, November 5, 1972
Cause: Gunfire

Wildlife Officer Leon Walker
Florida Game and Fresh Water Fish Commission
EOW: Thursday, August 13, 1970
Cause: Vehicle pursuit

Wildlife Officer Jimmy Thompson
Florida Game and Fresh Water Fish Commission
EOW: Tuesday, June 25, 1968
Cause: Electrocuted

Wildlife Officer Marvin J. Albritton
Florida Game and Fresh Water Fish Commission
EOW: Thursday, August 18, 1966
Cause: Accidental

Wildlife Officer Bud T. Smith
Florida Game and Fresh Water Fish Commission
EOW: Tuesday, November 30, 1954
Cause: Vehicle pursuit

Wildlife Officer Johnny Ingram
Florida Game and Fresh Water Fish Commission
EOW: Sunday, November 25, 1951
Cause: Aircraft accident

Wildlife Officer James R. Fields
Florida Game and Fresh Water Fish Commission
EOW: Sunday, December 24, 1950
Cause: Gunfire

Wildlife Officer Earl Sharp
Florida Game and Fresh Water Fish Commission
EOW: Wednesday, October 1, 1947
Cause: Aircraft accident

231

Made in the USA
Columbia, SC
13 January 2019